Coaching and Mentoring Skills

Andrew J. DuBrin
Rochester Institute of Technology

NETEFFECT SERIES

PEARSON

Prentice
Hall

Upper Saddle River, New Jersey

Library of Congress Cataloging-in-Publication Data

Dubrin, Andrew J.
  Coaching and mentoring skills / Andrew DuBrin.
      p. cm. — (NetEffect series)
  Includes bibliographical references and index.
  ISBN 0-13-092222-6
1. Mentoring in business. 2. Employees—Training of. 3. Employees—Counseling of.
4. Teams in the workplace. 5. Organizational behavior. 6. Interpersonal relations.
I. Title. II. Series.

HF5385.D8 2004
658.3'124—dc22   2004006562

Director of Production and Manufacturing: Bruce Johnson
Executive Editor: Elizabeth Sugg
Editorial Assistant: Cyrenne Bolt de Freitas
Marketing Manager: Leigh Ann Sims
Managing Editor—Production: Mary Carnis
Manufacturing Buyer: Ilene Sanford
Production Liaison: Denise Brown
Full-Service Production: Gay Pauley/Holcomb Hathaway
Composition: Carlisle Communications, Ltd.
Design Director: Cheryl Asherman
Senior Design Coordinator/Cover Design: Christopher Weigand
Cartoon Illustrations: David Watson

Pearson Education Ltd.
Pearson Education Australia Pty. Limited
Pearson Education Singapore Pte. Ltd.
Pearson Education North Asia Ltd.
Pearson Education Canada, Ltd.
Pearson Educatión de Mexico, S.A. de C.V.
Pearson Education—Japan
Pearson Education Malaysia Pte. Ltd.

ISBN 0-13-092222-6

Contents

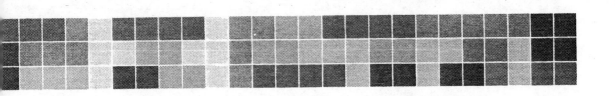

Overview

To achieve success in today's workplace, your involvement in coaching and mentoring activities is critical. Coaching and mentoring are more important than ever because they support the modern, team-based organization. It does not matter what position you hold in the company. More people work together as equals, and they are expected to train and develop one another. Coaching and mentoring facilitate such learning and also support the current emphasis on continuous learning.[1] Enabling workers to contribute more fully and productively to their jobs is now considered essential to corporate success. Coaching and mentoring serve as integral partnership builders in the corporate quest for innovation and improvement.

COACHING

You probably have some experience in coaching whether or not the activity was given a formal label. If you have helped someone else improve his or her performance on the job, on the athletic field, in a musical band, or on the dance floor, you have some coaching experience. In the workplace, **coaching** is a method of helping workers grow and improve their job competence by providing suggestions and encouragement. An effective coach displays the following skills and characteristics: empathy, active listening, ability to size up people, diplomacy and tact, patience toward people, concern for the welfare of others, self-confidence, noncompetitiveness with team members, and enthusiasm for people.

To understand what coaching truly involves, it is also helpful to understand what it does not. Several of these false stereotypes, as explained by Ian Cunningham and Linda Honold, follow:[2]

1. *Coaching applies only to one-to-one work.* In reality, the entire team or another group can also be coached. As a team member, or team leader, you might make a suggestion to the group, such as, "Why are we rushing through such an important issue?"

2. *Coaching is mostly about providing new knowledge and skills.* The truth is that people often need more help with underlying habits than with knowledge and skills. A good example is coaching another person about work habits and time management. You can provide the individual with loads of useful knowledge and techniques. If the person is a procrastinator, however, he or she must reduce procrastination before time management skills will help.

3. *Coaches need to be expert in something to coach.* To use a sports analogy, a good coach doesn't have to be or have been an outstanding athlete. An important role for the coach is to ask pertinent questions and listen. Questioning and listening can help the other person set realistic learning goals.

4. *Coaching has to be done face-to-face.* The face-to-face approach facilitates coaching. Nevertheless, telephone and email are useful alternatives when time and distance create barriers. A worker on a field trip, for example, might send his coworker/coach an email message asking, "The customer says that if I make a mistake with this installation, he'll never do business with us again. Any suggestions?"

MENTORING

Mentoring is also a method of helping others grow and develop, but it involves a greater range of helping activities and skills than coaching. In Homer's tale *The Odyssey*, Mentor was a wise and trusted friend as well as a counselor and adviser. A **mentor** is generally defined as an individual with advanced experience and knowledge who is committed to giving support and career advice to a less experienced person. The less experienced person is the **protégé** (from the French word for *protected*).

Mentoring is more important than ever because it supports the modern, team-based organization. Also, after years of downsizing, many organizations have fewer managers available to mentor employees. Coworkers often have to fill this void. More people work together as equals, and they are expected to train and develop each other. Mentoring facilitates such learning and also supports the current emphasis on continuous learning.

Mentoring has long been recognized as essential for advancing the careers of workforce members who are part of the majority group. Evidence gathered in recent years suggests that mentoring is also essential for the career advancement of minority group members.

As conducted by senior managers and coworkers, mentoring has become recognized as an important vehicle for the advancement of minorities in the workplace. A survey of successful minority executives indicated that 48 percent of the respondents said a role model had guided them toward early career goals. The role model/mentors were primarily of the same ethnic, racial, or cultural origin. A specific finding showed that successful minorities with supportive managers and coworkers have faster compensation growth and progress more rapidly in their firms. A sponsor of the survey said, "Minority executives believe that mentors are very helpful in advocating for upward mobility and teaching them how to navigate through the corporation."[3]

Mentoring is also gaining acceptance off the job. Many communities have developed programs whereby working adults volunteer to serve as mentors to youths. Mentoring in these programs is designed to help the adolescents and teenagers succeed at school and avoid lives of crime and substance abuse.

All mentors should be coaches and master the skills involved in effective coaching, but not all coaches need to be mentors. Any worker of any level can coach another team member. A mentor, however, is more experienced in some important aspect of the job and wiser than his or her protégé. Usually a mentor outranks the person he or she mentors and is older. The specific activities and skills involved in mentoring will be discussed more fully in Chapter 13, "Developing Protégés."

SUCCESSFUL COACHING AND MENTORING

It is not necessary to possess all the skills and characteristics of an effective coach to begin to coach or mentor. Like many leadership qualities and skills, these can be learned and developed with practice. This book describes and allows you to practice the skills needed to achieve success in your career as coach and mentor.

You do need to begin with the right mind-set, however, to properly absorb and learn these skills. You must be a nourishing, positive person to help others grow and develop. A **nurturing person** promotes the growth of others. Nurturing people are supportive and typically look for the good qualities in others. They recognize that most people have growth needs and want to help them with those needs. Being a nurturing, positive person is a lifelong process rather than a tactic that can be used at will. Nevertheless, making a conscious attempt to be nurturing and positive can help you develop the right mind-set.

Because the skills of coaching are necessary for both the successful coach and the effective mentor, this book is arranged so that we discuss those skills before further discussing the activities and skills of mentoring in their own chapters. There are 12 coaching skills (with corresponding chapters) that are critical for achieving success both for the coach or mentor and for the person being coached or mentored: (1) building trust, (2) showing empathy, (3) active listening, (4) using influence tactics, (5) helping others set goals, (6) monitoring performance, (7) giving feedback, (8) encouraging positive actions, (9) discouraging negative actions, (10) training team members, (11) helping others solve problems, and (12) helping difficult people. These skills intertwine and actually should be used to build upon each other.

YOUR COACHING AND MENTORING DIARY

Skill building exercises are presented throughout this book. A useful way of keeping track of your skill development and reinforcing what you learn is to maintain a diary of experiences related to sharpening your skills. You might organize your diary by chapters that correspond to the 13 chapters of this book. Keep note of the skills and understanding you develop. For example, an exercise might ask you to listen actively to what a coworker is saying. A suitable notation in you diary might be, "As I listened to Cynthia describing the technology problem she was facing, I looked carefully at how she bit her lips and tightened her jaw. I could tell she was really in pain about her problem. Now I know how important it is to use another person's body language to understand how he or she feels."

Notes

1. Erik J. Van Slyke and Bud Van Slyke, "Mentoring: A Results-Oriented Approach," *HRfocus* (February 1998), 14.
2. Ian Cunningham and Linda Honold, "Everyone Can Be a Coach," *HR Magazine* (June 1998), 63–66.
3. Jerry Langdon, "Minority Executives Benefit from Mentors," *Gannett News Service*, December 7, 1998. See also Letty C. Hardy, "Mentoring: A Long-Term Approach to Diversity," *HRfocus* (July 1998), S11.

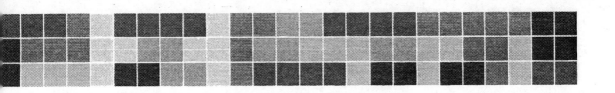

About the Author

An accomplished author, Andrew J. DuBrin, Ph.D., brings to his work years of research experience in business psychology. His research has been reported in *Entrepreneur*, *Psychology Today*, *The Wall Street Journal*, *Fortune*, *Small Biz*, and more than 100 other national magazines and local newspapers. An active speaker, Dr. DuBrin has appeared as a guest on over 350 radio and television shows. He has published numerous articles, textbooks, and well-publicized professional books. Dr. DuBrin received his Ph.D. from Michigan State University and is currently teaching leadership and organizational behavior at the Rochester Institute of Technology.

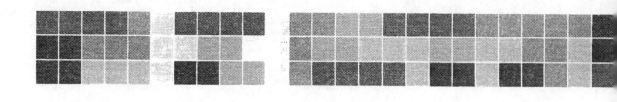

Acknowledgments

My thanks are extended to people who played a key role in producing *Coaching and Mentoring Skills* for career success. Valerie Munei assembled, integrated, and refined much of the information in the book. Elizabeth Sugg, assisted by Anita Rhodes, spearheaded the series in which this book appears. The production team at the Career, Health, Education and Technology Division of Pearson Education/Prentice Hall designed the book and helped convert ideas into a physical reality. Gay Pauley and Karen Swartz at Holcomb Hathaway also played key roles in the production of this book. Thanks also to readers of my previous books, without whom I would not have continued writing.

I would also like to thank the following reviewers who offered constructive suggestions: Diane Paul, TVI Community College; Kristopher Blanchard, North Central University; and Marnie Green, Management Education Group.

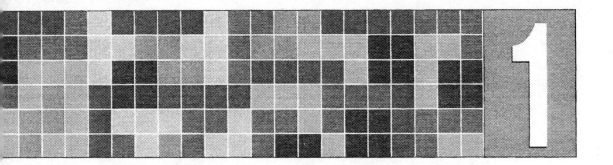

Building Trust

PERFORMANCE GOALS

After studying this chapter and doing the exercises, you should be able to:

- pinpoint what it means to be honest with people you coach and mentor.
- recognize how to demonstrate integrity.
- be credible with others.
- establish trust with team members, including your protégé.

"Nice to have a credible VP of Marketing."

UNDERSTANDING TRUST

As a coach and as a mentor, you can effectively help your team members and protégés grow only if they trust you. If you do not have their trust, you may not be allowed to help them. Gaining their trust earns you their respect, cooperation, and confidence.[1]

In this context, **trust** is defined as a person's confidence in another individual's intentions and motives and in the sincerity of that individual's words. To be trustworthy, you must display honesty, integrity, and credibility, and you must trust the people you're working with. A good coach/mentor **walks the talk,** thereby showing a consistency between deeds (walk) and words (talk). Hence you must develop your own trustworthy behaviors before you can help develop other people.

Trust is a delicate matter. It takes a coach or a mentor a long time to build trust; yet, one brief incident of untrustworthy behavior can destroy it. Examples of untrustworthy behavior would be using company money for private purposes or sexually harassing a team member. You may be allowed your fair share of honest mistakes. But if you make dishonest mistakes, you will quickly erode the trust of the person you are working with and your effectiveness as coach/mentor.

BUILDING TRUST

To gain the trust of the people you coach and mentor, you need to consistently demonstrate trustworthy behavior. You also need to be perceived as ethical so take the Ethical Reasoning Inventory.

1. Be Honest

Being honest is an effective way of getting others to trust you. **Honesty** involves telling the truth, being sincere, and not misleading or withholding information in relationships of trust. A starting point in developing a strong sense of honesty is to follow a variation of the Golden Rule: Be as honest with others as you want them to be with you.

2. Demonstrate Integrity

Integrity involves standing up for your beliefs about right and wrong and being your best self. A person who has integrity practices what he or she preaches regardless of pressure from others. In addition, integrity means keeping your promise, being fair to all people, being a good team player, and

---

ARE YOU READY?   The Ethical Reasoning Inventory

Directions: Describe how well you agree with each of the following statements. Use the following scale: disagree strongly (DS); disagree (D); neutral (N); agree (A); agree strongly (AS).

	DS	D	N	A	AS
1. When applying for a job, I would cover up the fact that I had been fired from my most recent job.	5	4	③	2	1
2. Cheating just a few dollars in one's favor on an expense account is OK if a person needs the money.	5	④	3	2	1
3. Employees should inform on each other for wrongdoing.	1	2	3	④	5
4. It is acceptable to give approximate figures for expense account items when one does not have all the receipts.	5	4	③	2	1
5. I see no problem with conducting a little personal business on company time.	5	4	③	2	1
6. Just to make a sale, I would stretch the truth about a delivery date.	5	4	3	②	1

Continued

7. I would fix up a purchasing agent with a date just to close a sale. 5 4 3 (2) 1

8. I would flirt with my boss just to get a bigger salary increase. 5 4 (3) 2 1

9. If I received $200 for doing some odd jobs, I would report it on my income tax return. 1 2 (3) 4 5

10. I see no harm in taking home a few office supplies. 5 4 3 (2) 1

11. It is acceptable to read the email messages and faxes of other workers, even when not invited to do so. (5) 4 3 2 1

12. It is unacceptable to call in sick in order to take a day off, even if only done once or twice a year. 1 2 (3) 4 5

13. I would accept a permanent, full-time job even if I knew I wanted the job for only six months. 5 4 3 (2) 1

14. I would first check company policy before accepting an expensive gift from a supplier. 1 2 (3) 4 5

15. To be successful in business, a person usually has to ignore ethics. 5 (4) 3 2 1

16. If I felt physically attracted toward a job candidate I would hire that person over a more qualified candidate. 5 (4) 3 2 1

17. On the job, I tell the truth all the time. 1 2 3 (4) 5

18. If a student were very pressed for time, it would be acceptable to either have a friend write the paper or purchase one. 5 (4) 3 2 1

19. I would authorize accepting an office machine on a 30-day trial period, even if I knew we had no intention of buying it. 5 (4) 3 2 1

20. I would never accept credit for a coworker's ideas. 1 2 3 (4) 5

Scoring and Interpretation: Add the numbers you have circled to obtain your total score.

90–100	You are a strongly ethical person who may take a little ribbing from coworkers for being too strait-laced.
66 60–89	You show an average degree of ethical awareness, and therefore should become more sensitive to ethical issues.
41–59	Your ethics are underdeveloped, but you at least have some awareness of ethical issues. You need to raise your level of awareness of ethical issues.
20–40	Your ethical values are far below contemporary standards in business. Begin a serious study of business ethics.

maintaining confidence. Remember that honesty and integrity are *not* the same. If you stick to your belief that lying to group members is acceptable behavior, you show integrity when you lie. Yet you are not honest. Karli, a department head, illustrates what integrity means in practice:

> Top management at Karli's company decided downsizing was necessary. To avoid any possible charges of favoritism, the people to be laid off would be those with average or below-average performance appraisals. Karli's manager asked her to give a below-average performance appraisal to Gus, a senior employee within the department. The boss said, "I know you think Gus is a good performer, but because of his lengthy service with the company his salary has climbed very high. If we downsize Gus, we can save a lot of money. But if he receives an above-average appraisal, he might complain that we laid him off because of his age. So, Karli, please do what needs to be done."
>
> Karli believed strongly that performance appraisals should be honest judgments about employees and not influenced by external factors. So she told her boss, "I am morally unable to lower Gus's appraisal just so he can be on the hit list. However, what I will do is rack my brain to find other ways to save the company money."

3. Develop Credibility

Credibility involves developing your emotional intelligence and communication skills, being open, being consistent, being knowledgeable and continually developing your work knowledge, and demonstrating competence in your technical and professional ability.

Credibility is based on the perceptions of others in two ways. First, people have to think you are telling the truth. Suppose you return from lunch and say, "Bill Gates and I were just contemplating the future of the PC industry over lunch. We will be continuing our dialog." Your coworkers might perceive you as being *incredible* (to say the least). Second, you have to convince others that you have enough solid knowledge and experience to carry out your role. A newly appointed high-school principal who had never taught in a classroom would not be perceived as credible by the faculty and staff. (If word got out to the students about the principal's lack of experience, he or she might have another credibility problem.)

4. Trust the Team

In effective coaching and mentoring, trust needs to be mutual. Trusting your team members and protégés also earns you their trust. To trust the people you coach or mentor, you must be willing to give up some control over them, such as letting group members make more decisions and not challenging their expense accounts.

Think It Through   The Trust Buster

Judy, a finance manager, was asked by her company to mentor Rick, a financial analyst who recently joined the company. The mentoring was part of a company program that matched new employees with experienced managers. The managers were to help newcomers in such ways as orienting them to the company, helping them solve problems, and assisting in guiding their careers.

Judy was lukewarm about the idea of having a protégé. She believed that time spent in mentoring would be time taken away from her more important responsibilities such as helping the company get a good return on its available cash. In Judy's words, "The best part of my day is when I'm at the computer searching for better yields on the company cash. I can actually make more money for the company than many sales reps. Besides, playing with money is as exciting to me as gambling at a casino."

When asked by her manager, the VP of finance, about her interest in mentoring Rick, she replied, "Great opportunity. I believe strongly in mentoring. My own career would not have been progressed as well as it has without one or two good mentors along the way. I'll do what I can for Rick."

Judy's first mentoring session with Rick went well. She invited him to lunch at one of her favorite restaurants where many finance specialists, including stockbrokers and investment bankers, dine. Rick was impressed with the ambiance. He noticed that many of the business-people seated at their tables were drinking wine, so Rick asked Judy if drinking at lunch was acceptable. Judy replied, "You want to act like a cool financial type, so go ahead and have a glass or two of wine. I'm not drinking today because this week I'm taking antihistamines for an allergy." During lunch, Judy talked in general terms about how she would be available to help Rick as needed.

Toward the end of the day, Sylvie, a coworker of Rick's, asked him how he enjoyed lunch with Judy. Rick explained that they visited a beautiful restaurant and that he drank two glasses of excellent Beaujolais. Sylvie replied, "Are you kidding? Don't you know that drinking at lunch is verboten in our company?" Rick was perplexed but thought that perhaps Judy was just going out of her way to make him feel comfortable in their first get-together.

A week later Rick approached Judy with a major question. He said he had observed that she had developed a reputation for attaining excellent returns on investment for the company's cash. "Could you please explain to me how you find short-term investments that beat the average so consistently?" Judy thought to herself, *Two weeks on the job, and this kid wants to know my best trade secrets. I'm his mentor, so I should tell Rick something of value, yet not give away all my secrets.*

Continued

"The subject is very complicated," answered Judy. "But I will get you started down the right track. At the start of every day, read *The Wall Street Journal,* both the print and on-line editions. I also have a few websites for professional investors I am going to recommend." Rick thanked Judy for the advice but felt he was receiving off-the-shelf information.

Ten days later Rick read an article about shadowing as part of mentoring. The article explained that shadowing is essentially following around a more experienced person for a workday to develop an in-depth understanding of how he or she performs the job. The next day, Rick sent an enthusiastic email message to Judy asking if he might be able to shadow her for a day, at her convenience. Judy thought about the email, and then replied, "Rick, shadowing is okay for learning a tangible skill like bike repair. It might not be as good for learning about finance management. Besides, I want to help you become an independent professional. If you follow me around for a day, it will foster dependency. Maybe you might shadow me during a meeting sometime."

Later that day, Ricardo, a financial analyst in the cubicle adjacent to Rick's, asked him how the mentoring program was going. Rick said with a smile, "First tell me Ricardo, how important do you think it is to trust your mentor?"

Questions

1. What is Judy doing that is creating a climate of distrust between her and Rick?
2. What should Judy do to improve her mentoring skills?
3. What is Judy doing right as a mentor?
4. Any advice to Rick for improving the mentoring he is receiving?

Summary

Establishing trust by being trustworthy is an important part of being an effective coach or mentor. Building trust can take a long time, but it can be achieved through (1) being honest, (2) demonstrating integrity, (3) developing credibility, and (4) trusting your team members and protégés.

Key Terms and Concepts

Credibility	Trust
Honesty	Walk the talk
Integrity	

How Do You Walk the Talk?

Walk the talk is a buzz term that has been popular in business and other types of organizations for at least 10 years. Like many clichés, the term is not particularly precise. A more accurate rendition would be *"implement your promises and expressed beliefs."* (However, I concede that *walk the talk* is catchier.) The idea is to show that you are serious about what you espouse and act as a model of the behavior you profess to be important. Here are a few positive examples of walking the talk:

- Marty, a financial consultant working for Northwestern Mutual, owns a $250,000 whole life policy.
- Sarah, a team leader of an industrial engineering group in a manufacturing firm, preaches squeezing the most productivity out of every work process. So she is always prompt for work at the start of the day, and at meetings. While waiting for complex files to download, she edits her to-do list.
- Matt, the CEO of a company with $50 million in annual sales, announces that the company is forced to downsize to earn enough profit to stay in business. So he lays off his personal assistant then votes himself a 30 percent salary reduction.
- Your own example of what you have done recently to *walk the talk*.

Expand Your View

Skill-Building Exercise: The Trust Fall

A standard part of outdoor training for team building and leadership is for people to experience being dependent upon other team members for their physical safety. One such trust builder is for a person to fall backward into the arms of teammates. If the person is not caught, he or she will sustain serious physical injury. (**Caution:** Excuse yourself from this exercise if you have a current injury, suffer from circulatory or eye disease, or are pregnant.)

The class organizes into groups of six. Each group member takes a turn standing on a chair (a blindfold is optional). At the appropriate signal from a team member, the person falls backward into the arms of teammates. The fall can take place outdoors on a lawn, on the beach, in the snow, or indoors in the classroom. After each person has taken a turn, discuss among yourselves the impact of this exercise on the development of trust. If time allows, conduct a class discussion of the advantages and disadvantages of the trust fall.

Questions

1. What can you do today to be perceived as even more trustworthy than you are perceived to be already?

2. Suppose you are perceived as being highly ethical and trustworthy. How will that help you in your career?

3. Several studies have shown that approximately one half of workers are cynical about the ethics and integrity of business leaders. What can business leaders do to regain the trust of employees?

4. A business professor was quoted in the newspaper as saying that about 99 percent of managers in business are honest, reliable people. Yet, the dishonest 1 percent get all the publicity for their poor ethics. What is your evaluation of the accuracy of this 99-to-1 ratio?

5. A widely circulated magazine geared toward entrepreneurs that had been published since 1891 recently went out of business. A substantial proportion of the articles in the magazine dealt with treating customers honestly and fairly. The magazine closed its website and left no phone number for subscribers to inquire about reimbursements for unfulfilled subscriptions. How might this magazine have behaved with better integrity and honesty?

6. When you first meet another person, which aspects of his or her physical appearance lead you to trust (or distrust) him or her?

7. A conflict of interest takes place when a person's objectivity is compromised. How can you avoid a conflict of interest with the person you are mentoring?

8. Illustrate how you can show a consistency between your words and actions in your line of work.

Notes

1. Stephen P. Robbins, *Organizational Behavior* (Upper Saddle River, NJ: Prentice Hall, 2001), 337–338.

Learning Links

Kesner, Idalene F. "The Coach Who Got Poached." *Harvard Business Review*, March 2002, 31–40.

Reinhold, Barbara. "Establishing Trust in the Workplace." http://content. monster.com.hk/managment/6866 (Accessed December 4, 2003).

Poe, Andrea. "Establish Positive Mentoring Relationships." *HR Magazine*, February 2002, 62–69.

Whitworth, Laura, Henry Kimsey-House, and Phil Sandahl. *Co-Active Coaching: New Skills for Coaching People Toward Success in Work and Life.* Palo Alto, CA: Davies-Black, 1998.

Showing Empathy

PERFORMANCE GOALS

After studying this chapter and doing the exercises, you should be able to:

- understand the meaning of empathy.
- develop more empathy for others on the job.
- demonstrate to others that you empathize with them.

"At least we will both be able to understand
what hard work is really like."

UNDERSTANDING EMPATHY

In order to help people grow and develop, it is essential that you understand the people you are coaching or mentoring, their interests and attitudes, and how to reach them. The more you know about them, the better
able you will be to deliver the messages you wish them to receive. This takes
empathy.

   Empathy is the ability to place yourself in the other person's shoes. Empathy does not necessarily mean that you sympathize with the other person. **Sympathy** means that you agree and understand. For example, you
may understand why some people are forced to beg in the streets, but you
may have very little sympathy for their plight. To empathize with another
person you don't have to agree, but you do have to understand.

   It is important to keep in mind that people perceive words and concepts
differently because their vantage points and perspectives differ. Such differences in **frame of reference** create barriers to communication. A frame of
reference can also be considered a lens through which we view the world.
A manager attempted to chastise a team member by saying, "If you keep up
your present level of performance, you'll be a repair technician all your life."
The technician replied, "That's good news," because he was proud of being

the first person in his family to hold a skilled job. Empathy can be considered an important communication bridge. If you understand another person's frame of reference, you will better receive and send messages and more effectively coach and mentor.

Empathy is also an important part of **active listening,** which will be discussed in the following chapter. Effective coaches and mentors listen intensely to their protégés with the goal of empathizing with them.

Effective coaches and mentors also go beyond using empathy to simply understand their team members or charges—they realize they must also demonstrate their empathy. Showing empathy is an essential relationship-building skill. When you show empathy, the person you are coaching or mentoring feels understood and accepted. This allows for more open communication and greater acceptance of what you have to say. It also earns trust.

DEVELOPING EMPATHY

To develop empathy you have to imagine yourself in the other person's role and assume the viewpoints and emotions of that individual. For example, if a supervisor were trying to communicate the importance of customer service to sales associates, the supervisor might ask himself or herself, "If I were a part-time employee being paid close to the minimum wage, how receptive would I be to messages about high-quality customer service?"

It is also important to develop the habit of looking to understand the feelings and emotions of people around you. When you have a hunch about people's motives, look for feedback to see if you were right.

SHOWING EMPATHY EFFECTIVELY

To be an effective coach or mentor, it is not enough to feel empathy for your team member or protégé; you must also demonstrate your empathy.

1. Use the Same Figures of Speech

An effective way of showing empathy is to accept and use the **figures of speech** of the person you are coaching. By so doing, the person feels understood and accepted. Also, if you reject his or her figure of speech by rewording it, the person you are coaching may become defensive. Many people use the figure of speech, "I'm stuck," when they cannot accomplish a task. You can facilitate smooth communication by a response such as, "What can I do to help you get unstuck?" If you respond with something like, "What can I do to help you think more clearly?" the person is forced to change mental channels and may become defensive.[1]

The following statements are designed to raise your awareness about your tendency to empathize with others. Check the appropriate column.

	Mostly True	Mostly False
1. If someone gives me a hard-luck story, I quickly tune out him or her.	☐	☑
2. I feel profoundly sorry for workers who lose their job during a downsizing.	☑	☐
3. I hate whiners.	☑	☐
4. When I am being criticized, I listen carefully to see if I can figure out what I am really doing wrong in the other person's eyes.	☑	☐
5. It is difficult for me to understand why a wealthy and well-known person would be unhappy.	☐	☑
6. It makes me sick when I find out that people in other countries actually eat animals we consider to be pets in my country.	☐	☑
7. Before sending an email message that I write, I review it carefully to reduce any possibility of the message being misunderstood.	☑	☑
8. I have little sympathy for people who see the world quite differently than I do.	☐	☑
9. I rarely change my mind after a heated discussion with another person.	☑	☐
10. Many people have said that I am a very understanding person.	☑	☐

Interpretation: The answers in the direction of having empathy are as follows: 1. Mostly False; 2. Mostly True; 3. Mostly False; 4. Mostly True; 5. Mostly False; 6. Mostly False; 7. Mostly True; 8. Mostly False; 9. Mostly False; 10. Mostly True.

You have an above-average degree of empathy if you scored 8, 9, or 10. You have average tendencies toward empathy if you scored 5, 6, or 7. You have below-average empathy if you scored 1, 2, 3, or 4.

ACTIVATE YOUR SKILLS: Developing Empathy for Differences

Class members come up to the front of the room one by one and give a brief presentation (perhaps even three minutes) of any way in which they have been perceived as different and how they felt about this perception. The difference can be of any kind, relating to characteristics such as ethnicity, race, choice of major, physical appearance, height, weight, hair color, or body piercing. After each member of the class (perhaps even the instructor) has presented, class members discuss what they learned from the exercise. It is also important to discuss how this exercise can improve relationships on the job.

ACTIVATE YOUR SKILLS: Practicing Empathy on the Job

The workplace is a natural setting for refining your empathy. Many people in your workplace probably toil away without other people ever wondering what it is like to occupy their role. Within the next two weeks enhance your empathy for the challenges faced by people who hold positions different from yours. In a friendly, good-natured way, ask three different workers questions such as those in the following list. Explain that you are attempting to improve your understanding of different types of work.

1. What's the biggest challenge you face in your job?
2. What does it take for you to have a really good day on the job?
3. How does your work help others?

After you complete each of these very brief interviews, jot down what you have learned. Ask yourself how your understanding of the jobs of others has improved. Make an entry in your coaching and mentoring diary of any skills this exercise has helped you develop.

2. Express Your Understanding

Another way to show empathy is to make sure you express your understanding of the other person's point of view before continuing your communication. As a team leader, you might ask a team member to work late one Thursday. The team member says, "That's my night to play bingo. Working is out of the question." You understand how important bingo is to that person, and you could begin with, "I know that you love playing bingo," before you move on to emphasizing the importance of the project.

Michael Daly's staff told him he needed to hire another dining-room helper to pour coffee at breakfast. But Daly, 38, the chief executive officer of a small chain of upscale retirement rental residences, wasn't buying it. Why hire someone else when the nursing aides could pitch in and serve? "I'm the CEO. I've got a big ego. I didn't believe it," he said.

That is until Daly, President of Sterling Glen Communities, ditched his suit and cell phone for a day on the job, following a work schedule set by the staff at Chancellor Park, a Philadelphia retirement home.

So far he has done his "Walking in Your Shoes Program" at two other of the company's nine facilities. When Daly reports for duty at 7 A.M., he has no idea what will be in store. "They want me to have the most difficult day possible," he said. Typically he works in the kitchen, handles a stint on the reception desks, empties trash, makes repairs, and cleans apartments. "They give me the dirtiest room, and I don't know how to clean a room," he said.

Daly said the work gives him a grass-roots knowledge of the facility, particularly when he manages to penetrate layers of middle management. His favorite spot for picking up knowledge is folding laundry with the housekeeping staff. Daly said it takes the crew about half an hour to loosen up enough to give him the lowdown.

At Chancellor Park, Daly's day started in the dining room, and that was when he saw how frantic it was. "I realized the aides were barely able to keep with the shower schedule. They couldn't pour coffee," he said. "We'll have to do something."

William Brown, executive director of Chancellor Park, said he would like Daly to authorize an additional maintenance worker. The last maintenance worker got so backed up that he left a big stack of work orders when he quit. Brown assigned Daly to complete four repair jobs in one hour and twenty minutes. It took Daly an hour longer, and he did not get everything done.

Daly visited Edith Creskoff, 94, who wanted the television moved in her apartment. "You're pretty efficient for a president," she said. Then it was on to Ron Polenz, a man in his 60s, who needed the hinges on his refrigerator door switched so he could open it from his wheelchair. "I had no idea they were reversible," Daly said. "I have to order 166 refrigerators, and now that I know, I'll make sure I order reversible ones."

Polenz watched Daly struggle to turn the refrigerator on its side as Daly muttered under his breath about not having the right tools for the job. "You're seeing my first bead of sweat of the day," Daly said.

I thought you were hot stuff already with that tool kit," Polenz joked before delivering his opinion of Daly's "Walking in Your Shoes" Program. "The man's the CEO, and he comes down

Continued

and sees for himself rather than wait for somebody to report to somebody else," said Polenz. "The more I think about it, the more I like the idea."

Source: "CEO Demotes Himself for a Day," Knight Ridder, September 23, 2002. Copyright © 2002/Knight Ridder/Tribute Media Services, Reprinted with permission.

Questions

1. In what way does this case history illustrate empathy?
2. How does the "Walking in Your Shoes" program help Daly become a leader?
3. How does the empathy Daly is developing extend beyond listening?

Summary

Empathy is the ability to place yourself in the other person's shoes. It does not necessarily mean that you agree with the other person; it does mean you have to understand the other person's point of view.

Empathy is an essential element in coaching and mentoring. It is an important goal in another coaching and mentoring skill: active listening. Empathy can be developed through imagining yourself taking another person's viewpoint and emotions.

To build relationships and better communication with the people you coach or mentor, you can show empathy by using their figures of speech and communicating your understanding of their points of view as you speak.

Key Terms and Concepts

Active listening
Empathy
Figure of speech

Frame of reference
Sympathy

Clarifying Differences in Paradigms Can Lead to Empathy

A method of understanding differences in frames of references is to recognize that people have different paradigms that influence how they interpret events. A **paradigm** is a model, framework, viewpoint, or perspective. Understanding another person's paradigm is another way of developing empathy for that person.

When two people look at a situation with different paradigms, a communication problem may occur. For instance, one person may say, "Let's go to Las Vegas for the computer show." The other person may respond, "A ridiculous idea. It costs too much money and takes too much time. Besides, the company would never approve." These objections are based on certain unstated beliefs:

- Air travel is the most suitable mode of transportation.
- Traveling over 500 miles a day by auto is fatiguing and dangerous.
- Traveling over a weekend for business and using vacation days cannot be considered seriously.
- Paying for such a trip with personal money is out of the question.

The other person has a different set of unstated beliefs:

- It is possible, traveling on interstate highways and using two drivers, to cover 1,000 miles in one day.
- Traveling over a weekend and taking vacation days is sensible.
- Paying for the trip with personal money is a sound educational investment.

The solution to this communication clash is to discuss the paradigms, thereby developing empathy. Both people live by different rules or guidelines (a major contributor to a paradigm). If the two people can recognize that they are operating with different paradigms, the chances for agreement are improved. When you demonstrate an understanding of the other person's paradigm, you are communicating empathy. Another benefit of discussing differences in paradigms is that people can shift their paradigms when the reasons are convincing.[2] For example, the second person in the preceding situation may never have thought about using personal funds for a trip as being an educational investment.

Expand Your View

Skill-Building Exercise: The Ultimate Empathy

Are you in the mood to stretch your empathy? To understand a perspective that is most likely very different from yours? This exercise will cost you about three dollars and will take a little time. The next time you are downtown in a large city purchase a copy of a newspaper called something like *The Street News* or *The Itinerant.* These newspapers are sold on the street by homeless people who earn a few dollars per day by selling the newspapers on commission plus tips. Homeless people or editors who share their point of view write the articles in these newspapers. Study carefully a few of the articles until you understand the lens through which a homeless person views the world. If the situation is appropriate, speak with the newspaper vendor for a few minutes with an eye toward understanding his (99 percent of the time) paradigm of the world.

A backup plan for this exercise if you do not have access to a big city is to ask somebody else who will be making such a visit to purchase the homeless-person newspaper. (You will need to find someone who can empathize with your task.)

This exercise will help develop your empathy because you are attempting to place yourself in the shoes of a person who is most likely walking a very different path than you. You can then take your sharply honed empathy to the office.

Questions

1. Why is empathy an important characteristic for a manager?
2. Why is empathy an important characteristic for a sales representative?
3. Describe a difference in *frame of reference* that you have had with another person.
4. In what way does being a good listener improve a person's ability to empathize with others?
5. In what way can you send the message to another person that you have empathy for him or her?
6. How might showing empathy for another person help you reduce conflict with him or her?
7. Give an example of how a customer service representative might show empathy for a customer's problem.

Notes

1. Daniel Araoz, "Right-Brain Management (RBM): Part 2," *Human Resources Forum* (September 1989), 4.
2. Suzette Haden Elgin, *Genderspeak* (New York: Wiley, 1993).

Learning Links

Terez, Tom. "Remember, They're *Human* Resources." *Workforce,* January 2002, 22–24.

Understand Differences, Develop Empathy to Communicate Better. www.advancingwomen.com/workplace/empathy.html (accessed December 4, 2003).

Zachary, Lois J. *The Mentor's Guide: Facilitating Effective Learning Relationships.* San Francisco: Jossey-Bass, 2000.

Active Listening

PERFORMANCE GOALS

After studying this chapter and doing the exercises, you should be able to:

- comprehend the essence of active listening.
- avoid distraction, establish good eye contact, and let the other person speak.
- listen for both fact and feelings and acknowledge what is being said.
- ask good questions and be open to learning from the people you coach or mentor.
- smile appropriately when listening.

"Keep talking, I'm listening."

UNDERSTANDING ACTIVE LISTENING

Listening is an essential ingredient in any coaching or mentoring session. Unless you receive messages as they are intended, you cannot effectively perform your job as coach or mentor. Effective listening improves your relationships with your protégés because people listen to feel understood and respected. Furthermore, coaches and mentors cannot identify the problems your team members experience unless you listen carefully to them.

A major component of effective listening is to be an active listener. As we mentioned in the previous chapter, the active listener listens intensely with the goal of empathizing with the speaker. As a result of listening actively, the listener can feed back to the speaker what he or she thinks the speaker meant.

Listening takes hard work and commitment. As a result of being a listener, the coach/mentor will be able to see and summarize the progress of the person he or she is working with as well as to provide better emotional and task-related support and encouragement to that person.

LISTENING ACTIVELY

You can listen more effectively by carefully utilizing the steps that follow.

Communication specialists at Purdue University have identified certain behavior patterns that interfere with effective hearing and listening. After thinking carefully about each trap, check how well the trap applies to you: "Not a problem," or "Need improvement." To respond to the statements accurately, visualize how you acted when you were recently in a situation calling for listening.

	Not a Problem	Needs Improvement
1. *Mind reader.* You will receive limited information if you constantly think, "What is this person really thinking or feeling?"	☑	☐
2. *Rehearser.* Your mental rehearsals for "Here's what I'll say next" tune out the sender.	☑	☐
3. *Filterer.* You engage in selective listening by hearing only what you want to hear. (Could be difficult to judge because the process is often unconscious.)	☑	☐
4. *Dreamer.* You drift off during a face-to-face conversation, which often leads you to an embarrassing "What did you say?" or "Could you repeat that?"	☐	☑
5. *Identifier.* If you refer everything you hear to your experience, you probably did not really listen to what was said.	☑	☐
6. *Comparer.* When you get sidetracked sizing up the sender, you are sure to miss the message.	☑	☐
7. *Derailer.* You change the subject too quickly, giving the impression that you are not interested in anything the sender has to say.	☑	☐
8. *Sparrer.* You hear what is said, but quickly belittle or discount it, putting you in the same class as the derailer.	☑	☐
9. *Placater.* You agree with everything you hear just to be nice or to avoid conflict. By behaving this way, you miss out on the opportunity for authentic dialogue.	☑	☐

Interpretation: If you checked "Need Improvement" for five or more of the above statements, you are correct—your listening needs improvement! If you checked only two or fewer of the above traps, you are probably an effective listener and a supportive person.

Source: Reprinted with permission from *Message: The Communication Skills Book* (Oakland, CA: New Harbinger Publications, 1983).

1. Avoid Distraction

If feasible, keep papers and your computer screen out of sight when listening to somebody else. These kinds of distractions tempt you to glance away from the message sender. In an age when multitasking is so common, it is difficult to remember to focus on the listener. Act as if every word the message sender delivers is vitally important. Listen as if you were a counselor being paid to hear the message sender's problems. Or imagine that your software is stuck and that you are patiently listening to a help technician walk you through the necessary steps to get up and running. Listening is hard work.

2. Establish Good Eye Contact

At the start of your conversation, notice the other person's eye color to help you establish eye contact (But don't keep staring at his or her eyes!). During the conversation, continue to maintain eye contact most of the time. To avoid rigid behavior take "eye breaks" to glance to the side or upward. Cupping your chin in your hand will tilt your head in a manner that suggests you are carefully reflecting on the message while maintaining partial eye contact. After your eye break, return to a direct gaze.

Establishing eye contact is important because it helps you concentrate and therefore listen better. Maintaining eye contact also communicates respect and caring.

3. Let the Person Speak

Be patient about waiting your turn to speak. A common barrier to effective listening is to mentally prepare an answer while another person is speaking. The coach or mentor should not be poised for a rebuttal. Keep your ratio of talking to listening down to about 1 to 5. In other words, spend 20 percent of your time talking and 80 percent listening.

Many people have difficulty allowing the other person to speak because silence makes them uncomfortable. The inexperienced listener will jump in with conversation to fill a silence. Professional listeners, such as business coaches, remain silent and wait for the other person to talk. Within about 30 seconds of silence, the other person will begin talking. He or she also will become a little anxious under the pressure of silence. Don't worry. You are not playing mind games; you are using advanced listening skills.

4. Listen for both Fact and Feelings

An active listener tries to grasp both facts and feelings. Observing your protégé's nonverbal communication is part of active listening. When a person speaks, too often we listen to the facts and ignore the feelings. If feelings are ignored, the true meaning and intent of the message are likely to be missed. Imagine you are coaching Jim, to whom you have just assigned ten new accounts. Jim says, "Okay, I will now take on ten of the accounts that Carol was handling before she quit." The statement suggests that Jim accepts the idea that he now has ten new accounts. But if you dig a little deeper, Jim's feelings will be evident, as follows:

> **You:** Yes, you have ten new accounts, but how do you feel about it?
>
> **Jim:** I'm worried because I'm already handling more than my fair share of accounts. The company is unwilling to hire a replacement for Carol, so I have to take over half her accounts.
>
> **You:** Jim, you're telling me that ten new accounts are too much for you. Let's talk about how you might better organize your work.

5. Use Body Language Effectively

Body language is an important part of active listening for both the receiver and sender of the message. Indicate by your body language that you are listening intently. When a coworker comes to you with a question or concern, focus on the person and exclude all else. If you grasp at your cell phone or glance around the room, you send the message that the other person does not warrant your full attention.

Be sensitive to the body language of the person to whom you are listening. Do the person's facial expressions jibe with the words spoken? For example, does the person claim to want to help you with a project yet frowns, bites the lips, and fidgets? In this case the person's body language would suggest that he or she does not really want to help you. Worse, if the person does help you, he or she might do a poor job. On the other hand, does the person project a warm smile and have a relaxed posture when talking about wanting to help you? If so, the message sent may be more authentic.

6. Listen for Understanding

Remember to be empathetic and follow the **LUNA rule:** Listen for Understanding, Not Agreement. The person you are coaching may have a very different viewpoint from yours. If you listen to understand, you will encourage your protégé to understand your point of view. Ask gentle—not confrontational—questions that enhance your ability to understand. Let's get back to your work with Jim. Instead of telling him that he could easily handle ten more accounts if he were better organized, you listen to understand *why* ten new accounts might be difficult for him to manage:

> **You:** What are you concerns about taking on ten of Carol's accounts?
>
> **Jim:** I want to do a good job with the 27 accounts I already have. If I take on ten new accounts, my workdays will be frantic. I'll be stressed out.
>
> **You:** I understand you better now, Jim. It's a workload issue. Maybe I can give you a few suggestions to ease the stress of managing so many accounts.

7. Acknowledge What is Being Said

Let your team member or protégé know you're listening by nodding your head in agreement from time to time. Perhaps mutter "mmh" or "uh-huh" periodically but not incessantly.

Reflect the speaker's feelings. Reflection-of-feeling responses typically begin with "You feel that . . . "

Reflect the speaker's content or meaning. The active listener **paraphrases,** or repeats in his or her own words what the team member or protégé says, feels, and means.

Summarize concisely what is being said. **Summarization** involves pulling together and condensing and thereby clarifying the main points communicated by the other person. You might say, "What I heard you say during our meeting is that . . . " or, "As I understand it, your position is that . . . "

8. Ask Good Questions

Ask open-ended questions to encourage your team member or protégé to talk about his or her performance. Open-ended questions facilitate a flow of conversation. For example, ask, "How did you feel about the way you handled conflict with the marketing group yesterday?" A close-ended question covering the same issue would be, "Do you think you could have done a better job of handling conflict with the marketing group yesterday?" Closed questions do not provide the same opportunity for self-expression, and they often elicit short, uninformative answers. The latter question would not provide good clues to specific problems faced by your coworker. Suppose the person you are coaching is late with an assignment. Instead of saying, "I must have your assignment by Thursday afternoon," try "When will I get your assignment?"

9. Be Open to Learning from the People you Coach or Mentor

Even though you may have more experience than your team member or person you mentor in some areas, there may be things he or she can teach you. Ask yourself whether anything the other person is saying could benefit you.

Maintaining this perspective will enable you to benefit from most listening episodes and will motivate you to listen intently.

Being open to the suggestions of people you are coaching fits in with the modern approach to management that recognizes the importance of input from workers directly involved with products, services, and customers. A trucking company manager, for example, listened to his trucker who said, "I know the company is emphasizing being the fastest in the business. But our customers don't care so much about speed. What they want to know is whether we deliver the goods when we said we would and without being damaged." The company then saved money by learning what was truly important to customers. Delivering at breakneck speed was less important than simply meeting promises and delivering with care.

10. Smile Appropriately

A final suggestion is not to smile continuously during your conversation. Although you may appear friendly, the smiling could also be interpreted as your not taking the other person seriously.[1] It is difficult to precisely establish the percentage of time that the listener should be smiling, so it is best to analyze what types of comments merit a smile. Among the best reasons for smiling are:

You agree strongly with the message sender.

The message sender smiles at you.

The message sender compliments you.

The message sender says something you perceive to be witty.

The message sender gets the point of a complex idea that you are
explaining.

A rough guide is that smiling somewhere between 25 percent and 35 percent of the time will communicate the message that you are a warm person yet that you do not think everything is humorous.

Think It Through   The Financial Services Coach

Kristine Florentine is an account representative (stockbroker) at a branch office of a financial services firm. Her manager, Chad Olsen, is concerned that Kristine is 25 percent below quota in sales of a new hedge mutual fund offered by the company. (In the past, *hedge funds* were only for the richest investors.) Chad sets up an appointment with Kristine to spur her to achieve quota. The conversation proceeds, in part, in this manner:

Olsen: My most important responsibility is to help team members work up to their
potential. I wanted to get together with you today to see if there is any way I can

Continued

help you. During the last quarter you were 25 percent below quota in your sales of our new hedge fund. That displeases me as well as top management because our profit margin on this fund is very high.

Florentine: I know that I'm under quota, but I can't help it. It's just tough pushing a hedge fund these days. Our clients are getting conservative, and they don't want to jump into an investment they don't understand well that is associated with taking a high risk.

Olsen: Why don't your clients understand the hedge fund?

Florentine: It's a new fund, so they don't understand it. The information I send them is pretty complicated for a layperson.

Olsen: What steps could you take to make this fund easier for our clients and prospects to understand?

Florentine: Maybe I could work up a thirty-second presentation that would give a nice overview of the hedge fund. This would enable me to make a quick pitch over the phone. I could back it up with more details by email.

Olsen: Now you're making good sense. But I'm disappointed that an intelligent person like you didn't think of that before. Do you have a self-confidence problem when it comes to making quota on a new product?

Florentine: Most people would have a self-confidence problem if they were going through what I am these days. It's not that easy concentrating on my work.

Olsen: I don't like to hear excuses, but I'll make an exception this time. What are you going through that makes it difficult for you to concentrate on your work, Kristine?

Florentine: My sister and I are pretty close, and she's in big trouble. I mean *big* trouble. She was down on her luck, so she started dealing in drugs. I warned her. My folks warned her, but she wouldn't listen. She got busted recently and faces a ten-year prison term.

Olsen: Sorry to hear about your sister. But why feel so down? You weren't involved in her drug dealing, were you?

Florentine: What's really dragging me down is that my sister used to tell me that I was her model. Her ideal. Some ideal. Her life is ruined.

Olsen: Now I understand why you are so down. However, let's meet again real soon to talk about your sales on the hedge fund.

1. Identify the strengths in Olsen's listening technique.
2. Identify the areas for improvement in Olsen's listening technique.
3. How effective is Olsen as a coach?

Summary

Listening is the key to building relationships with your protégés. It helps you show respect for the people you coach, mentor, or both. It helps you identify the areas of improvement you and your team member need to work on together.

Active listening enables you to provide the support and encouragement the person you coach or mentor may need. You can use several techniques to listen actively including: (1) avoiding distraction, (2) establishing good eye contact, (3) letting the person speak, (4) listening for both fact and feelings, (5) using body language effectively, (6) listening for understanding, (7) acknowledging what is being said, (8) asking good questions, (9) being open to learning from the people you coach or mentor, and (10) smiling appropriately.

Key Terms and Concepts

Asking good questions   Paraphrasing
LUNA rule   Summarization

Expand Your View

Skill-Building Exercise: Listening to a Protégé

Restating what you hear (summarization) is particularly important when listening to a person who is talking about an emotional topic.

■ *The elated protégée.* One student plays the role of a protégée who has just been offered a promotion to supervisor of another department. She will be receiving a 10 percent raise in pay and be able to travel overseas twice a year for the company. She is eager to describe full details of her good fortune to her mentor. Another student plays the role of the mentor to whom the protégée charge wants to describe her good fortune. The mentor decides to listen intently to his or her charge. Other class members will rate the mentor on his or her listening ability.

■ *The discouraged protégé.* One student plays the role of the employee who has just been placed on probation for poor job performance. His boss thinks that his performance is below standard and that his attendance and punctuality are poor. He is afraid that if he tells his girlfriend, she will leave him. He is eager to tell his tale of woe to his

The Importance of Listening to the Team[2]

Judy George is chair and CEO of Boston-based Domain Home Fashions, a company with 250 employees. She learned about the importance of listening to team members the hard way. George, age 60, was fired from her last company—after building revenue from $2 million to $100 million in seven years—because she stepped on everybody's toes. "I treated everybody as if they were all Judy Georges running around. I thought enthusiasm was contagious. After I was fired, I began to realize that not everybody operated the same way I did," she says. After the trauma of being fired settled down, George reflected that she should look for the good in what workers are saying or doing, even if their thoughts and actions were different from hers.

When George founded Domain in 1985, she made certain to hire people who didn't share her personality traits—and she promised herself that she would listen to them. The change helped the business thrive, she says. When she wanted to launch a website for selling furniture several years ago, for instance, her managers persuaded her that the company was not ready to handle returns.

Net shoppers typically take a try-it-and-see approach. If a buyer in Sante Fe didn't like a sofa, Domain would have been saddled with the costs of warehousing it out West or shipping it back to the manufacturer. "This is why, after five years, no major furniture company is making money on-line," says George. "If we had done what I wanted to do, we would have lost a fortune. But I learned to listen to my team."

mentor. Another student plays the role of the mentor to discuss his problems. The mentor decides to listen intently to the employee's problems but is pressed for time. Other class members will rate the mentor on his or her listening ability.

Make entries in your coaching and mentoring diary about what you learned.

Questions
1. Why is summarization such a powerful communication technique?
2. Professional listeners, such as psychotherapists, note frequently that they are exhausted after listening to patients for a few hours. Why is listening so exhausting?

3. Many companies have found that training employees in listening provides a good return on investment. How can better listening lead to increased sales or cost savings?

4. What is the difference between *hearing* and *listening*?

5. What benefit would a deaf person derive from having studied this information about more effective listening?

6. Why is it that experienced interviewers ask relatively few questions in comparison to inexperienced interviewers?

7. Give an example from your own life in which careful listening helped you accomplish an assignment well.

Notes

1. "Train Yourself in the Art of Listening," *Positive Leadership*, sample issue (Summer 2000), 10.

2. Adapted from Margaret Littman, "Best Bosses Tell All," *Working Woman*, (October 2000), 51–52, www.domainhomefashions.com.

Learning Links

Exercise Four: Active Listening. http://crs.uvm.edu/gopher/nerl/personal/comm/e.html (accessed December 4, 2003).

Teerez, Tom. "Can We Talk?" *Workforce*, July 2000, 46–55.

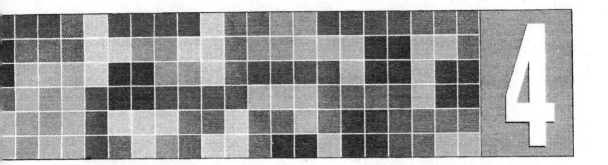

Using Influence Tactics

PERFORMANCE GOALS

After studying this chapter and doing the exercises, you should be able to:

- recognize the difference between an ethical and an unethical influence tactic.

- influence others by being a role model and using persuasion.

- influence others by being assertive and displaying humor.

- enhance your charisma.

"We are truly like a team of Navy Seals. We take on the toughest, the dirtiest, and the most dangerous assignments. And we win almost all the time!"

UNDERSTANDING INFLUENCE

Influence is the ability to affect the behavior of others in a particular direction. As a coach or as a mentor, influencing others is your basic responsibility. Generally, influence tactics are discussed in relation to leaders. Whether or not you have formal authority in your role as coach or mentor, you are expected to lead your team members and persons you mentor to worthwhile objectives. Therefore, the more leadership skills you develop, the more positive outcomes you will have with your team members and protégés.

Influence tactics in themselves can be ethical and honest or manipulative or dishonest. To establish strong, positive, and trustworthy relationships with your team members, ethical and honest strategies of influence work best.

USING ETHICAL INFLUENCE TACTICS

Five ethical influence tactics can be highlighted that contribute to effective coaching and mentoring.

1. Be a Role Model

As a coach or mentor, your team members and protégés look to you for guidance and leadership. They will generally take your lead on how to behave and act. They will more often do what you do than what you tell them to do. So it is critical that you do as you want them to do. This may take some self-analysis and self-development to accomplish.

ARE YOU READY?   The Positive-Impression Survey

Directions: Please indicate how often you use the following ways of impressing work associates, including customers. Use the following ratings: 1 = Very infrequently (VI); 2 = Infrequently (I); 3 = Sometimes (S); 4 = Frequently (F); and 5 = Very frequently (VF). Circle the most accurate answer.

Tactic or Method	VI	I	S	F	VF
1. Dressing well	1	2	3	4	5
2. Making a favorable appearance other than through dress	1	2	3	4	5
3. Using colorful speech	1	2	3	4	5
4. Being cheerful	1	2	3	4	5
5. Appearing self-confident	1	2	3	4	5
6. Being neat and orderly	1	2	3	4	5
7. Pretending to others that I am in demand	1	2	3	4	5
8. Talking about quality as it relates to the job	1	2	3	4	5
9. Talking about own accomplishments	1	2	3	4	5
10. Being knowledgeable about the topic at hand	1	2	3	4	5
11. Achieving high job performance	1	2	3	4	5
12. Creating a problem and then solving it to look good	1	2	3	4	5
13. Talking about team play	1	2	3	4	5
14. Being diplomatic	1	2	3	4	5
15. Sharing expertise with others	1	2	3	4	5
16. Sharing credit with others	1	2	3	4	5
17. Giving warmth and support	1	2	3	4	5
18. Following through with promises	1	2	3	4	5
19. Exaggerating my accomplishments	1	2	3	4	5
20. Saying what other person wants to hear	1	2	3	4	5
21. Listening carefully	1	2	3	4	5

Continued

22. Making small talk	1	2	3	4	5
23. Talking about work	1	2	3	4	5
24. Showing good ethics	1	2	3	4	5
25. Sending greeting cards to work associates	1	2	3	4	5
26. Avoiding a direct "No" in dealing with others	1	2	3	4	5
27. Being calm under pressure	1	2	3	4	5
28. Flattering others	1	2	3	4	5

Interpretation: This questionnaire is not designed to provide a score. Instead, compare your frequency ratings to a group of 300 men and women holding a variety of managerial, sales, and professional jobs. The following mean scores refer to ratings on the 1-to-5 scale.

1. Dressing well, 4.1
2. Favorable appearance, 4.3
3. Colorful speech, 3.6
4. Cheerfulness, 4.3
5. Self-confident appearance, 4.5
6. Neatness, 4.2
7. Pretending to be in demand, 2.0
8. Talk of quality, 4.2
9. Talk of accomplishments, 2.6
10. Knowledge of topic, 4.2
11. High performance, 4.7
12. Creating problems, 1.8
13. Team player talk, 3.6
14. Diplomacy, 4.0
15. Share expertise, 4.2
16. Share credit, 3.9
17. Warmth and support, 4.1
18. Following through, 4.4
19. Exaggeration, 2.0
20. Saying what people want to hear, 2.7
21. Listening, 4.1
22. Small talk, 3.0
23. Work talk, 3.3
24. Ethics display, 4.4
25. Greeting cards, 2.6
26. Avoid direct "No," 3.1
27. Pressure handling, 4.1
28. Flattery, 0.9

Your rating of the impression-management tactics may provide useful clues to skill development. If you use a given tactic much less frequently than others, you might consider evaluating whether you are using this tactic enough. For example, if you make very infrequent use of warmth and support to impress others, you might increase the frequency of such behavior to the norm (4.1 = frequently). In other instances, you might decide that you are overusing a tactic (such as exaggerating).

Note: In the comparison groups, only one statistically significant difference was found between men and women in the use of these impression tactics. Women gave a mean frequency rating of 2.9 for the use of greeting cards, while men gave a frequency rating of 2.3.

Source: Andrew J. DuBrin, "Sex Differences in the Use and Effectiveness of Tactics of Impression Management," *Psychological Reports,* vol. 74, 1994, 531–544.

As a **role model,** you give your team members and persons you mentor a pattern of values and behaviors to emulate. You actually help them develop this way. Among the many factors that make you role-model material are a strong work ethic, job expertise, personal warmth, good speaking ability, a professional appearance, and great ethics.

You can also model an example of desired behaviors in specific situations. A customer service manager was harsh with customers when facing heavy pressure. One way the supervisor coached the service manager was by taking over the manager's desk during a busy period. The service manager then watched the supervisor deal tactfully with demanding customers.

2. Use Persuasion

Persuading your team members and charges to follow your suggestions is a powerful influence tactic. You can use this tactic both in writing and in speaking. **Persuasion** involves convincing someone to accept his or her message—in other words, selling your idea to others. Some **persuasive communication** techniques are described next.

Techniques for Persuasive Communication[1]

■ *Know exactly what you want.* Your chances of selling an idea increase to the extent that you have clarified the idea in your own mind. The clearer and more committed you are at the outset, the stronger you are as a persuader.

■ *Never suggest an action without telling its end benefit.* A team member or protégé is more likely to take the action you suggest if you explain its benefit.

■ *Phrase your proposition in terms of the receiver's interests.* The basic rule of selling is an extension of the communication strategy "understand the receiver." People are far more likely to accept your idea if it is clear how they will benefit. Most receivers want to know "What's in it for me?"

▧ *Explore the reasons for people's objections.* This is an effective strategy to empathize with the person you are coaching or mentoring. When you understand his or her concerns, you will also be able to address them as you work to get the team member or protégé to accept your suggestion.

■ *Get a yes response early on.* It is helpful to give the selling session a positive tone by establishing a "yes pattern" at the outset.

■ *Use power words.* An expert tactic for being persuasive is to sprinkle your speech with **power words** (meaning *powerful* words). Power words stir emotion and bring forth images of exciting events. Examples of power words include *decimating* the competition, *bonding* with customers, *surpassing* previous profits, *capturing* customer loyalty, and *rebounding* from a downturn.

■ *Minimize raising your pitch at the end of sentences.* Part of being persuasive is to not sound unsure and apologetic. In English and several other languages, a convenient way to ask a question or to express doubt is to raise the pitch of your voice at the end of a sentence or phrase. As a test, use the sentence "You like my ideas." First say *ideas* using approximately the same pitch and tone as with every other word. Then say the same sentence by pronouncing *ideas* with a higher pitch and louder tone. By saying *ideas* loudly, you sound much less certain and are less persuasive.

■ *Avoid or minimize common language errors.* You will enhance your persuasiveness if you minimize common language errors, because you will appear more articulate and informed. An example of a common language error is to say "Me and my coworker" instead of "My coworker and I."

3. Be Assertive

A widely recognized leadership trait is **assertiveness,** or being forthright in expressing demands, opinions, feelings, and attitudes. The assertive person lets others know how he or she feels, partly by expressing emotion. An assertive mentor, for example, might say, "I am so excited about that proposal for cost reduction you are submitting to management next week. I think it's a real winner."

If you are self-confident, it is easier to be assertive with people. Being assertive will help you be a more effective coach and mentor. You will be able to confront team members and protégés about their mistakes, demand higher performance, and set high expectations. You will also be able to make legitimate demands on higher management, such as asking for equipment needed by the group.

The accompanying skill-building exercise will help you develop your assertiveness.

4. Show Humor

Humor can relieve tension and defuse hostility. Because humor helps the coach or mentor dissolve tension and defuse conflict, it helps him or her exert power over the group. A study conducted in a large Canadian financial institution indicated that leaders who made frequent use of humor had higher-performing units. (Another interpretation is that it's easier to laugh when the group is performing well!) You can use humor to take the edge off during stressful periods and help team members or protégés laugh at themselves.[2]

The most effective form of humor is tied to the situation. It is much less effective for you to tell rehearsed jokes. A key advantage of a witty, work-related comment is that it indicates mental alertness. A canned joke is much more likely to fall flat.

Directions: Indicate whether each of the following statements is mostly true or mostly false as it applies to you. If in doubt about your reaction to a particular statement, think of how you would generally respond.

	Mostly True	Mostly False
1. It is extremely difficult for me to turn down a sales representative when that individual is a nice person.	☐	☐
2. I express criticism freely.	☐	☐
3. If another person were being very unfair, I would bring it to his or her attention.	☐	☐
4. Work is no place to let your feelings show.	☐	☐
5. No use asking for favors; people get what they deserve.	☐	☐
6. Business is not the place for tact; say what you think.	☐	☐
7. If a person looked as if he or she were in a hurry, I would let that person in front of me in a supermarket line.	☐	☐
8. A weakness of mine is that I'm too nice a person.	☐	☐
9. I usually give other people what they want rather than do what I think is best, just to avoid an argument.	☐	☐
10. If the mood strikes me, I will laugh out loud in public.	☐	☐
11. People would describe me as too outspoken.	☐	☐
12. I am quite willing to return merchandise that I find has a minor blemish.	☐	☐
13. I dread having to express anger toward a coworker.	☐	☐
14. People often say that I'm too reserved and emotionally controlled.	☐	☐
15. Nice guys and gals finish last in business.	☐	☐
16. I fight for my rights down to the last detail.	☐	☐
17. I have no misgivings about returning an overcoat to the store if it doesn't fit me right.	☐	☐
18. After I have an argument with a person, I try to avoid him or her.	☐	☐
19. I insist on my spouse (or roommate or partner) doing his or her fair share of undesirable chores.	☐	☐

Continued

20. It is difficult for me to look directly at another person when the two of us are in disagreement. ☐ ☐

21. I have cried among friends more than once. ☐ ☐

22. If someone near me at a movie kept up a conversation with another person, I would ask him or her to stop. ☐ ☐

23. I am able to turn down social engagements with people I do not particularly care for. ☐ ☐

24. It is in poor taste to express what you really feel about another individual. ☐ ☐

25. I sometimes show my anger by swearing at or belittling another person. ☐ ☐

26. I am reluctant to speak up at a meeting. ☐ ☐

27. I find it relatively easy to ask friends for small favors such as giving me a ride to work while my car is being repaired. ☐ ☐

28. If another person were talking very loudly in a restaurant and it bothered me, I would inform that person. ☐ ☐

29. I often finish other people's sentences for them. ☐ ☐

30. It is relatively easy for me to express love and affection toward another person. ☐ ☐

Scoring Key

1. Mostly false	11. Mostly true	21. Mostly true
2. Mostly true	12. Mostly true	22. Mostly true
3. Mostly true	13. Mostly false	23. Mostly true
4. Mostly false	14. Mostly false	24. Mostly false
5. Mostly false	15. Mostly true	25. Mostly true
6. Mostly true	16. Mostly true	26. Mostly false
7. Mostly false	17. Mostly true	27. Mostly true
8. Mostly false	18. Mostly false	28. Mostly true
9. Mostly false	19. Mostly true	29. Mostly true
10. Mostly true	20. Mostly false	30. Mostly true

Interpretation: Score yourself a plus one (+1) for each of your answers that agrees with the scoring key. If your score is 15 or less, it is probable that you are currently nonassertive. A score of 16 through 24 suggests that you are assertive. A score of 25 or higher suggests that you are aggressive. Retake this quiz about 30 days from now to give yourself some indication of the stability of your answers. You might also discuss your answers with a close friend to determine whether that person has a similar perception of your assertiveness.

ACTIVATE YOUR SKILLS: Decisiveness Leads to Assertiveness

An important part of being assertive is to be decisive. To enhance your decisiveness, follow these steps:

1. Make a list of the requests people make of you that are a burden. Review the list and select one or two requests that you will refuse in the next week. Think about how you will politely, but firmly, inform someone of your need to say "no." Then carry out your plan. What happened? Did you feel less guilty than you thought you would?

2. Review the requests you want to make of others to help you meet your own needs. Select one or two. Get clear in your mind what you specifically want. Formulate each request so that it is as reasonable as possible for the person you will ask, then make your request(s). Did you get a positive response? Are you happy with the support you obtained?

3. Make an entry into your coaching and mentoring diary as to the success of your efforts in enhancing your assertiveness.

Source: Adapted from Mel Silberman, with Freda Hansburg, *PeopleSmart: Developing Your Interpersonal Intelligence* (San Francisco: Berrett-Koehler Publishers, 2000), pp. 90–91.

Self-effacing humor can also be an effective coaching and mentoring technique. When you are self-effacing, nobody else is insulted or slighted, yet a point can be made. A vice president of human resources at CISCO Systems said a few years ago, "I want you people to create an employee self-service system for inquiring about benefits so uncomplicated that I could learn to use it." Creativity is required for humor. Just as creativity can be enhanced with practice, so can a sense of humor.

5. Develop Charisma

Charisma, a type of charm and magnetism that inspires others, can help you motivate those you coach or mentor to greater achievement. Possessing a naturally dynamic personality is a major contributor to charisma, but you can engage in many tangible actions that also contribute to charisma. Here are a number of suggestions for behaving charismatically.

Techniques for Developing Charisma

▪ *Communicate a vision.* A charismatic leader offers an exciting image of where the organization is headed and how to get there. A vision is more

ACTIVATE YOUR SKILLS: The Witty Leader

Groups of about five students gather in problem-solving teams to invent humorous comments a leader might make in the following scenarios. After the problem-solving groups have formulated their witty comments, the comments can be shared and compared. Groups also have the option of deciding that a particular scenario is too grim for humor.

- *Scenario 1:* A store manager wants to communicate to employees how bad business has been lately. Sales have declined about 20 percent for three consecutive weeks.

- *Scenario 2:* A leader has to communicate to the group that salaries have been frozen for another year due to limited business. The leader knows that group members have been eagerly awaiting news about a salary increase.

- *Scenario 3:* Due to an unprecedented surge in orders, all salaried personnel will be required to work about 65 hours per week for the next 10 weeks. Furthermore, the office and factory must be staffed on Saturdays and Sundays.

- *Scenario 4:* A consulting firm that specializes in helping companies downsize their workforce has seen the demand for their services decline substantially in recent months. The company must therefore downsize itself. The company founder has to announce the layoff decision to the company.

than a forecast because it describes an ideal version of the future of an entire organization or an organizational unit such as a department.

- *Make frequent use of metaphors and analogies.* To inspire people, the charismatic leader uses colorful language and exciting metaphors and analogies. Develop metaphors to inspire people around you. A commonly used one after a group has suffered a setback is, "Like the phoenix, we will rise from the ashes of defeat." To pick up the spirits of her maintenance group, a maintenance supervisor told the group, "We're a lot like the heating and cooling system in a house. A lot of people don't give us much thought, but without us their lives would be very uncomfortable."

- *Be highly energetic and goal oriented.* Impress your team members and protégés with your energy and resourcefulness. To increase your energy supply, exercise frequently, eat well, and get ample rest. Be optimistic about

ARE YOU READY? How Important Do I Make People Feel?

Indicate on a 1-to-5 scale how frequently you act (or would act if the situation presented itself) in the ways indicated below: very infrequently (*VI*); infrequently (*I*); sometimes (*S*); frequently (*F*); very frequently (*VF*). Circle the number underneath the column that best fits your answer.

	VI	I	S	F	VF
1. I do my best to correctly pronounce a coworker's name.	1	2	3	4	5
2. I avoid letting other people's egos get too big.	5	4	3	2	1
3. I brag to others about the accomplishments of my coworkers.	1	2	3	4	5
4. I recognize the birthdays of friends in a tangible way.	1	2	3	4	5
5. It makes me anxious to listen to others brag about their accomplishments.	5	4	3	2	1
6. After hearing that a friend has done something outstanding, I shake his or her hand.	1	2	3	4	5
7. If a friend or coworker recently received a degree or certificate, I would offer my congratulations.	1	2	3	4	5
8. If a friend or coworker finished second in a contest, I would inquire why he or she did not finish first.	5	4	3	2	1
9. If a coworker showed me how to do something, I would compliment that person's skill.	1	2	3	4	5
10. When a coworker starts bragging about a family member's accomplishments, I do not respond.	5	4	3	2	1

Scoring and Interpretation: Total the numbers corresponding to your answers. Scoring 40 to 50 points suggests that you typically make people feel important; 16 to 39 points suggests that you have a moderate tendency toward making others feel important: 10 to 15 points suggests that you need to develop skill in making others feel important. Study this chapter carefully.

what you and the group can accomplish. People associate optimism with energy. Being grumpy is often associated with being low on energy. You can also add to an image of energy by raising and lowering your voice frequently, and avoiding a slow pace.

▪ *Be emotionally expressive and warm.* A key characteristic of charismatic leaders is the ability to express feelings openly. In dealing with team members and protégés, refer to your feelings at the time, such as, "I'm excited because I know we are going to hit our year-end target by mid-October." Nonverbal emotional expressiveness, such as warm gestures and frequent touching (nonsexual) of the people you coach or mentor, also exhibits charisma.

■ *Make ample use of true stories.* An excellent way of building rapport is to tell stories that deliver a message.[3] People like to hear stories about how a department or company went through hard times when it started, such as how Dell Computer began in a dormitory room at the University of Texas. Telling positive stories has become a widely accepted technique for building relationships with employees. Storytelling adds a touch of warmth to the teller and helps build connections among people who become familiar with the same story.

■ *Smile frequently, even if you are not in a happy mood.* A warm smile seems to indicate a confident, caring person, which contributes to a perception of charisma.[4]

■ *Be candid.* Practice saying what you want directly, rather than being indirect and evasive. If you want someone to help you, don't ask, "Are you busy?" Instead ask, "Can you help me with a problem I'm having right now?"

■ *Make everybody you meet feel that he or she is important.* For example, at a company social gathering, shake the hand of every person you meet. Also frequently thank your team members and persons you are mentoring both orally and by writing notes.

■ *Multiply the effectiveness of your handshake.* Shake firmly without creating pain, and make enough eye contact to notice the color of the other person's eyes. When you take that much trouble, you project care and concern.

■ *Stand up straight and use other nonverbal signals of self-confidence.* Practice good posture. Minimize fidgeting, scratching, foot tapping, and speaking in a monotone. Walk at a rapid pace without appearing to be panicked. Dress fashionably without going to the extreme that people notice your clothes more than they notice you.

■ *Be willing to take personal risks.* Charismatic leaders are typically risk takers, and risk taking adds to their charisma. Risks you might take would include extending additional credit to a start-up business, suggesting a bright but costly idea, and recommending that a former felon be given a chance in your firm.

■ *Be self-promotional.* Charismatic leaders are not shy. Instead, they toot their own horns and allow others to know how important they are (thereby being assertive). Without appearing self-absorbed, you, too, might let others know of your tangible accomplishments. Explain to others the key role that you played on your team or how you achieved a few tough goals.

Twenty-seven-year-old Colleen McFerguson worked as a merchandising specialist for ValuMart, one of the largest international retail chains. Based in the United States, ValuMart also has a strong presence in Canada, Europe, Japan, and Hong Kong. Colleen began her employment with ValuMart as a cashier, and two years later she was invited into the training program for merchandising specialists.

Colleen performed well as a merchandising trainee in the soft-goods line. Her specialty areas included men's, women's, and children's clothing, linens and bedding, men's and women's jewelry, and home decorations. For several years in a row, Colleen received performance evaluation ratings of above average or outstanding. Among the write-in comments made by her supervisors were "diligent worker," "knows the tricks of merchandising," "good flair for buying the right products at the right price," and "fits right into the team."

Despite the positive performance appraisals supported with positive comments, Colleen had a gnawing discontent about her career at ValuMart. Despite five years of good performance, she was still not invited to become a member of the ValuTrackers, a group of merchandising and operations specialists who are regarded as being on the fast track to becoming future ValuMart leaders. The leaders hold high-level positions such as head merchandiser, regional vice president, and store manager.

Several times when Colleen inquired about why she was not invited to join the ValuTrackers, she was told that she was not quite ready to be included in this elite group. She was also told not to be discouraged because the company still valued her contribution.

One day Colleen thought to herself, "I'm heading toward age 30, and I want a great future in the retail business now." So she convinced her boss, merchandising supervisor Evan Tyler, to set up a career conference with three people: Colleen, the boss, and her boss's boss, Heather Bridges, the area merchandising manager. She let Evan know in advance that she wanted to talk about her potential for promotion.

Evan started the meeting by saying, "Colleen, perhaps you can tell Heather and me again why you requested this meeting."

Colleen responded, "Thanks for asking, Evan. As I mentioned before, I'm wondering what you think is wrong with me. I receive a lot of positive feedback about my performance, but I'm not a ValuTracker. Also, you seem to change the subject when I talk about wanting to become a merchandising supervisor and eventually a merchandising executive. What am I doing wrong?"

Heather responded, "Evan and I frequently talk about the performance and potential of all our merchandising specialists. You're a good performer, Colleen, but you lack that little spark

Continued

45

that makes a person a leader. You go about your job efficiently and quietly, but that's not enough. We want future leaders of ValuMart to make an impact."

Evan added, "I go along with Heather's comments. Another point, Colleen, is that you rarely take the initiative to suggest ideas. I was a little shocked by your request for a three-way career interview because it's one of the few initiatives you have taken. You're generally pretty laid back."

"Then what do I have to do to convince you two that I should be a ValuTracker?" asked Colleen.

Heather replied, "Start acting more like a leader. Be more charismatic." Evan nodded in agreement.

Questions

1. What career advice can you offer Colleen McFerguson?
2. What might Colleen do to develop more charisma?
3. What is your opinion of the fairness of the ValuTracker program?

Summary

As a coach or as a mentor, it is your basic responsibility to influence your team members and protégés to accomplish worthwhile objectives. Effective and ethical influence tactics include (1) providing a role model, (2) using persuasion, (3) being assertive, (4) showing humor, and (5) developing charisma.

Key Terms and Concepts

Assertiveness	Persuasion
Charisma	Persuasive communication
Humor	Power words
Influence	Role model

Expand Your View

Skill-Building Exercise: Creating a Vision

The class organizes into small problem-solving groups. Each group constructs a vision for a unit of an organization or for a total organization of its choos-

More Insight into the Nature of Charisma

Charismatic leadership results from a group of behaviors and traits that create the attribution of being charismatic.[5] A key characteristic of charismatic leaders is their vision. They offer a vision (or lofty goal) of where the organization is headed and how to get there (a plan). A sense of vision inspires employees to perform well. For example, CEO Andrea Jung of Avon Products wants the company to become the "ultimate relationship marketer of products and services for women and the source for anything and everything a woman wants to buy."[6]

Charismatic leaders are masterful communicators. They formulate believable dreams and portray their vision of the future as the only path to follow. Leaders who are charismatic also use metaphors to inspire people. An example is a favorite of Richard Marcus, president of Neiman-Marcus stores: "If you follow in someone else's footsteps, you never get ahead." An underlying reason charismatic leaders communicate so well is that they are emotionally expressive. They readily express how they feel, which also enables them to form close ties with people.

Charismatic leaders at their best inspire trust. Quite often their constituents are willing to gamble with their careers to follow the chief's vision. Another behavior of charismatic leaders is helping group members feel capable. One technique they use is letting their people achieve success on relatively easy projects. They praise their people and then give them more demanding assignments. Charismatic leaders are energetic and use an action-oriented leadership style. They exude energy, serving as a model for getting things done well and on time. An extreme example is Richard Branson of the Virgin Group, including Virgin Atlantic Airways and about 100 other businesses. Branson spreads himself thin with some personal involvement in all these businesses. He also leads a daredevil lifestyle with such stunts as riding hot air balloons and sliding down a large pole in Times Square, New York, to promote a new store.

Branson's flamboyant behavior illustrates another key characteristic of charismatic leaders: They purposely manage their impressions and promote themselves. They package information about themselves to look good, and they pay careful attention to their appearance. A charismatic person often drops hints about the influential people he or she knows and brings personal accomplishments to the attention of others.[7]

Some aspects of charisma are related to basic personality factors such as extraversion. Nevertheless, it is possible for most people to enhance their charisma (as described earlier).

ing. Students can choose an organization with which they are familiar or a well-known business firm or government agency. The vision should be approximately 25 words long and depict a glorious future. A vision is not simply a straightforward goal, such as "In 2008 our firm will gross $10 million in sales." Remember, the vision statement you draw should inspire people throughout the organization.

Questions

1. Should a person use power words when he or she is not in a power job?
2. Can you provide an example of something a leader motivated or inspired you to do that you would not have done without his or her presence?
3. Identify three areas in life in which being charismatic would help a person achieve his or her goals.
4. Why is charisma an important characteristic for an effective coach?
5. Why are rehearsed jokes less effective than spontaneous humor as an influence tactic?
6. Identify three of the most common language errors you have heard.
7. Identify a business leader who you think is charismatic. What is the basis for your conclusion?

Notes

1. Jimmy Calano and Jeff Salzman, "Persuasiveness: Make It Your Power Booster," *Working Woman* (October 1988), 124–125; Roberta H. Krapels and Vanessa D. Arnold, "Speaker Credibility in Persuasive Work Situations," *Business Education Forum* (December 1997), 25; Gayle Theiss, "Say It Smart," *Aspire* (November–December 1998), 3–4.
2. Bruce J. Avolio, Jane M. Howell, and John J. Sosik, "A Funny Thing Happened on the Way to the Bottom Line: Humor as a Moderator of Leadership Style Effects," *Academy of Management Journal*, (April 1999), 219–227.
3. Elizabeth Weil, "Every Leader Tells a Story," www.fastcompany.com/online/15/rftf.html (accessed May 6, 1999).
4. Suggestions 7, 9, and 10 are from Roger Dawson, *Secrets of Power Persuasion* (Upper Saddle River, NJ: Prentice Hall, 1992), 181–183.
5. Jay A. Conger and Rabindra N. Kanugo, *Charismatic Leadership in Organizations* (Thousand Oaks, CA: Sage, 1998).
6. Nanette Byrnes, "Avon: The New Calling," *Business Week*, (September 18, 2000), 139.
7. William L. Gardner and Bruce J. Avolio, "The Charismatic Relationship: A Dramaturgical Perspective," *Academy of Management Review*, (January 1998), 32–58.

Learning Links

Eckert, Robert A. "Where Leadership Starts." *Harvard Business Review*, November 2001, 53–62.

Goffee, Robert, and Gareth Jones. "Why Should Anyone Be Led by You?" *Harvard Business Review*, September–October 2000, 62–70.

Useem, Michael. "The Leadership Lessons of Mount Everest." *Harvard Business Review*, October 2001, 51–58.

Helping Others
Set Goals

PERFORMANCE GOALS

After studying this chapter and doing the exercises, you should be able to:

- enhance goal setting by reviewing or developing a mission statement.
- help others establish specific and realistic goals and assign deadlines to goals.
- periodically review the relevance of goals.
- provide support to the goal setter.

"It's great to be working for a company that believes in goals."

UNDERSTANDING GOAL SETTING

A **goal** is an event, circumstance, object, or condition a person strives to attain. You are probably familiar with goal-setting techniques in your own professional and personal life. Applying that knowledge and experience to help your team members and protégés achieve company and professional goals will generate successful outcomes for you and your group.

Goal setting is well accepted as a motivational tool. Substantial research indicates that setting specific, reasonably difficult goals improves performance.[1] Goals in coaching and mentoring are useful for several reasons. First, goals focus your team members' efforts in a consistent direction.

Second, goal setting increases the chance for success, particularly because success can be defined as the achievement of a goal. The goals we set for accomplishing a task can serve as a standard to indicate when we have done a satisfactory job.

Third, goals serve as self-motivators and energizers. People who set goals show motivation and confidence because their energy is being invested in something worthwhile. Aside from helping you and the people you coach or mentor become more motivated and productive, setting goals can help both you and your team members and protégés achieve personal satisfaction. Most people derive a sense of satisfaction from attaining a goal that is meaningful to them.

Goals in the coaching situation may be somewhat different from those in the mentoring situation. As a coach, especially in a supervisory position, you should encourage the development of goals that are linked to the overall mission of the company. As a mentor, you may help your charge to set more career-oriented or personally oriented goals.

The skill of helping others set goals is also useful in setting performance standards (as will be discussed in Chapter 6), encouraging positive actions (as will be discussed in Chapter 8), and training others (as will be discussed in Chapter 10).

HELPING OTHERS SET GOALS

Effective coaches and mentors need to make sure the people they coach and mentor know and use the principles of goal setting. To do this you can lead your team members or protégés through a systematic approach.

1. Review or Develop a Mission Statement

A mission propels the goal setter toward being productive. The mission serves as a compass to direct your team member's activities, such as being well organized in order to attain a favorable performance appraisal. Stephen Covey, a popularizer of time management techniques, expresses the importance of a mission and goals in his phrase, "Begin with the end in mind."[2]

For the team member, the **mission statement** for his or her goals could be developed from the company's, department's, or work team's mission statement. For the protégé, the mission statement may be generated from a major lifetime goal.

The mission statement for the group helps answer the question, "Why are we doing this?" To answer the question, the mission statement should contain a specific goal, purpose, and philosophical tone. Any goal contained within the mission statement should be congruent with organizational objectives—what the company is trying to achieve. If the team wants to improve customer service, that should be part of the organization's intent also. Here are three examples of team mission statements:

- To plan and implement new manufacturing approaches to enhance our high-performance image and bolster our competitive edge.
- To enhance our website development capability so we can provide decision makers throughout the organization with assistance in developing websites that exceed the state of the art.
- To be the envy of the company in terms of delivering on-time, top-quality maintenance service.

ARE YOU READY?   Are You Ready for Goal Setting?

Answer each of the following questions spontaneously and candidly. As with all self-help quizzes, if you try to answer the question in a way that will put you in a favorable light, you will miss some potentially valuable diagnostic information. For each question, answer 1 for strongly disagree, 2 for disagree, 3 for a neutral attitude, 4 for agree, and 5 for strongly agree.

1. I almost always know what day of the month it is.   _____
2. I regularly prepare to-do lists.   _____
3. I make good use of my to-do lists.   _____
4. I can tell you almost precisely how many times I engaged in my favorite sport or hobby this year.   _____
5. I keep close tabs on the win and lose record of my favorite athletic team.   _____
6. I have a reasonably accurate idea of the different income tax brackets.   _____
7. I use a budget to control my personal expenses.   _____
8. I know how much money I want to be making in five years.   _____
9. I know what position I want to hold in five years.   _____
10. Careful planning is required to accomplish anything of value.   _____

                                                            Total   _____

Scoring and Interpretation: Add up your point score. If your score is 40 points or higher, you are probably already convinced of the value of goal setting. If your score is between 20 and 39 points, you are in the middle range of readiness to incorporate goal setting into your life. You probably need to study more about goal setting to capitalize on its value. If your score is between 10 and 19 points, you are far from ready to accept goal setting. Carefully review the information about the advantages of goal setting mentioned previously. Until you change your attitudes about the contribution of goals to your life, you will not become an active goal setter and planner.

You, as the team leader, can specify the mission when the team is first formed or at any other time. Developing a mission for a long-standing team breathes new life into its activities. Being committed to a mission improves teamwork, as does the process of formulating a mission. It's fun to talk about your purpose in the company. The dialogue necessary for developing a clearly articulated mission establishes a climate in which team members can express feelings. In this way, they feel they are participating in decisions of significance.

2. Establish Specific and Realistic Goals

Goals are more specific than mission statements. The goals support the mission statement. The coach/mentor should work with his or her team member or protégé to write down specific and realistic goals.

A useful, specific goal can usually be expressed in a short, punchy statement. An example: "Decrease input errors in bank statements so that customer complaints are reduced by 25 percent by September 30 of this year." People new to goal setting typically commit the error of formulating lengthy, rambling goal statements. These lengthy goals involve so many different activities that they fail to serve as specific guides to action. As a coach, you need to review the goal statement with your team member to ensure the goal helps focus his or her actions.

A realistic goal represents the right amount of challenge for the person pursuing the goal. On the one hand, easy goals are not very motivational—they may not spring the goal setter into action. On the other hand, goals that are too far beyond the capabilities of the goal setter may lead to frustration and despair because of a good chance for failure. The extent to which a goal is realistic depends on a person's capabilities. An easy goal for an experienced person might be a realistic goal for a beginner. The role of the coach in the step is to diplomatically and tactfully encourage team members to set goals within their capabilities.

3. Set Deadlines

Goals are best set for different time periods, such as daily, short-range, medium-range, and long-range goals. Daily goals are essentially a to-do list. Short-range goals cover the period from approximately one week to one year. Medium-range goals relate to events that will take place within perhaps two to five years. Long-range goals refer to events taking place five years into the future and beyond.

Setting specific time limits for goals encourages action and commitment. **Deadlines** also allow for you and the person you are coaching to measure his or her performance. Your role as coach is to help the goal setter distinguish when the goal can and should be achieved and then set realistic deadlines for that goal.

4. Develop an Action Plan

An **action plan** describes how you are going to reach your goal. The major reason an action plan is needed for most goals is that without a method for achieving the desired result, the goal is likely to slip by. Few people ever prepare a road map or plan that will lead them to their goals. If your goal were to build your own log cabin, part of your action plan would be to learn how to operate a buzz saw, how to build a log cabin, how to operate a tractor, and so forth. The coach should ensure that the goal setter develops an action plan that encourages success.

Some goals are so difficult to reach that the action plan might encompass hundreds of separate activities. Separate action plans would then have to be developed for each step of the way. The coach should help the goal setter reevaluate and break down such difficult goals.

Some immediate goals do not really require an action plan. A mere statement of the goal may point to an obvious action plan. If your goal were to start painting your room, it would not be necessary to draw up a formal action plan such as; "Go to hardware store, purchase paint, brush, and rollers; borrow ladder and drop cloth from Ken; and put furniture in center of room."

5. Review Goals from Time to Time

A sophisticated goal setter realizes that all goals are temporary to some extent. In time, one particular goal may lose its relevance and therefore may no longer motivate. The coach should help the goal setter monitor this situation. If an old goal is related to the performance appraisal of the employee, delete or replace or establish new goals as necessary.

6. Provide Support to the Goal Setter

The coach offers more than developing goals. If possible, he or she can provide the proper tools, equipment, and human resources to accomplish objectives of the team member. The coach can also help team members by reducing barriers to getting work accomplished. Most importantly, an effective coach looks out for the satisfaction of the team. Small things sometimes mean a lot in terms of personal satisfaction. Providing emotional support is another way of improving worker satisfaction. An emotionally supportive coach would engage in activities such as listening to team members' problems and offering them **encouragement** and praise. (For more on listening, see Chapter 3, "Active Listening." For more on encouragement, see Chapter 8, "Encouraging Positive Actions.")

7. Set Goals for the Group or Team as Well as Individuals

Having employees work as teams with specific team goals, rather than as individuals with only individual goals, increases productivity. It also reinforces the importance of working together as a team. Furthermore, the

Think It Through   Motivating the Kitchen Staff at the Blue Gardenia

Jimmy Gomez aspires to someday be the manager of a large hotel. To help work toward that goal he is working part-time on a degree in food and hotel administration. He attends classes at various times to fit his demanding full-time position as the kitchen staff supervisor at the Blue Gardenia, a well-established downtown hotel. Gomez supervises a staff of about 45 kitchen workers, including food preparers, butchers, bakers, and cooks. The highly paid chefs report to the restaurant manager, Sonya Rosato, who is also Gomez's manager.

The average wage is $8.00 per hour for the kitchen staff reporting to Gomez. Half of these workers work part-time and receive almost no benefits. The full-time staff receive a few modest benefits, such as vacation, a $20,000 life insurance policy, and medical insurance. Blue Gardenia management believes strongly that they pay competitive wages for kitchen staff and that paying them much more would eat into profits too much. During a goal-setting conference with Rosato, Gomez agreed that an important area for improvement in his operation would be to reduce turnover and increase productivity among the kitchen staff. Rosato pointed out that although the turnover rate for Jimmy's employees was about average for kitchen staff in the geographic area (75 percent per year), it was still too high. If the turnover rate could be trimmed down to about 45 percent, it would save the hotel thousands of dollars in hiring and training costs. In addition, less food would be wasted because trainees make so many mistakes in food preparation. Skilled workers also drop fewer dishes and glasses.

Rosato and Gomez also agreed that lower turnover would mean more kitchen staff would have good job skills and would therefore be able to produce more. For example, a skilled salad-maker can make twice as many salads as a beginner. Another concern Rosato expressed was that many of the kitchen staff seemed lazy.

During the week following the meeting with his boss, Gomez kept thinking about the problem. He decided tentatively that he was really dealing with a motivational issue. Jimmy reasoned that if the staff were better motivated, they would stay with the job longer and obviously should not appear lazy. As a starting point in attempting to better motivate the kitchen staff, he conducted a few informal interviews with them during breaks and toward the end of the workday. Jimmy asked 12 of the kitchen workers what Blue Gardenia management could do to keep kitchen staff on the job longer and working harder. A few of the comments Jimmy collected were as follows:

"What do you expect for eight dollars an hour? Some kind of superman? I work as hard as a factory worker, but I don't get paid like a factory worker."

"This is like a dead-end job. If I could find a job with a better future, I'd be out of here in no time."

Continued

"I like this job fine. But just like a few of the other guys here, I've got a problem. My wife and I are expecting a child. If I stay in this job, I won't be able to support my child. My wife wants to drop out of work for a year to care for the baby."

"Not me, but I think some of the workers here think management doesn't care much about them. So if they can find another job that pays even twenty-five cents more per hour, they're gone."

"I like this kind of work. I mean, we're really doing some good. People like nice entertainment, and eating good food is a form of entertainment. Also, we're keeping people healthy and helping them live longer. Our food is made with the best ingredients. Even the beef we prepare is lean and healthy."

"My gripe is not with the work, but that we don't get enough respect. The chef gets the glory, but we do a lot of the real work. I think I'm doing important work, but nobody tells me I am. Sometimes I think I'm treated like just another piece of kitchen equipment. A few of the other guys and gals feel the same way about how they're treated."

After the interviews were completed, Jimmy thought to himself that he had a lot of information. Yet he wondered how he could translate all this information into an action plan that would reduce turnover and keep the kitchen staff working harder.

Questions

1. What goals has Sonya Rosato established for Jimmy Gomez?
2. How might Gomez use goal setting to motivate his staff toward less turnover?
3. In what way do the thoughts expressed by the kitchen staff suggest goals the staff might be pursuing—even if not directly stated?

combination of compatible group and individual goals is more effective than either individual or group goals. Here are two examples of group goals:

- Reduce the accident rate from two accidents per 1000 employee work hours to one accident per 2000 employee work hours within twelve months.
- Increase repeat business from 35 percent of customers to 50 percent within one year.

Summary

Helping those you coach and mentor set goals is an important skill in motivating and developing them. Goal setting also has other applications in setting performance standards, encouraging positive actions, and training others. The coach/mentor best helps others set goals working with them through the following steps: (1) reviewing the company or department mission statement or developing a mission statement with the person being coached or mentored, (2) establishing specific and realistic goals for that mission, (3) setting a deadline for each goal, (4) developing an action plan to achieve the goal, (5) reviewing goals from time to time, and (6) providing support to the goal setter.

Key Terms and Concepts

Action plan	Goal
Deadline	Goal setting
Encouragement	Mission statement

The Potential Downside of Goal Setting

Goals are such an integral part of businesses, not-for-profit firms, and personal life that few people stop and think of the potential hazards of goals. Although we believe that setting and attaining goals contribute immensely to accomplishment and happiness, it is worth examining what can go wrong with goals. A major problem is that *goals can create inflexibility.* People can become so focused on reaching particular goals that they fail to react to emergencies, such as neglecting a much-needed machine repair in order to achieve quota.

Goals can contribute to a *narrow focus, thereby causing the person to neglect worthwhile activities and opportunities.* A sales representative might neglect to invest time in cultivating a prospective big customer because of a pressure to make quota. Instead, the sales rep goes for the quick sale with an established customer. (The company can fix this problem by making the cultivation of new business a high-priority goal.)

Another problem is that *performance goals can sometimes detract from an interest in the task.* People with a performance-goal orientation (focusing on being judged as competent) will sometimes lose interest in the task, especially a difficult one. However, if a person's goal orientation is primarily to learn a new skill, the person will not be readily frustrated when he or she encounters a problem.

Consider also that *goals can interfere with relaxation.* A preoccupation with goals makes it difficult to relax. Instead of improving one's life, goals then become a source of stress. If the person is already under pressure, taking on another goal may be overwhelming.

Expand Your View

Skill-Building Exercise 1: Goal-Setting and Action Plan Worksheet

Before writing down your goals, consult the section, "Helping Others Set Goals." If you are not currently employed, set up hypothetical goals and action plans for a future job.

Long-Range Goals (beyond five years)

Work: _____

   Action plan: _____

Personal: _____

   Action plan: _____

Medium-Range Goals (two to five years)

Work: _____

   Action plan: _____

Personal: _____

   Action plan: _____

Short-Range Goals (within two years)

Work: _____

   Action plan: _____

Personal: _____

   Action plan: _____

Skill-Building Exercise 2: Goal Sharing and Feedback

Each person selects one work-related and one personal goal from the Goal-Setting and Action Plan Worksheet that he or she would be willing to share with other class members. In turn, every class member presents those two goals to the rest of the class exactly as they are stated on the worksheet. Other class members have the opportunity to provide feedback to the person sharing his or her goals. Here are a few types of errors commonly made in goal setting that you should avoid:

1. Is the goal much too lengthy and complicated? Is it really a number of goals rather than one specific goal?

2. Is the goal so vague that the person will be hard-pressed to know if he or she has reached the goal (e.g., "I intend to become a good worker")?

3. Is the action plan specific enough to serve as a useful path for reaching that goal?

4. Does the goal sound sincere? (Admittedly, this is a highly subjective judgment on your part.)

Questions

1. How can people who are not sure what field they want to enter, nevertheless set long-range goals?
2. What is the relationship between a mission and a goal?
3. How useful are goals in mentoring another person?
4. How useful are goals in coaching another person?
5. Why is a vision really a type of goal?
6. Give an example of how any employer of yours set goals.
7. What is your most important goal?

Notes

1. Edwin A. Locke and Gary P. Latham, *A Theory of Goal Setting and Task Performance* (Upper Saddle River, NJ: Prentice Hall, 1990), 27–62.
2. Stephen R. Covey with Elaine Pofeldt, "Why Is This Man Smiling?" *Success*, (January 2000), 38–40.

Learning Links

Camarati, Jeff. "The Coach K Difference." *Success*, February/March 2001, 28–33.
www.topachievement.com/goalsetting.html
Vandewalle, Don. "Goal Orientation: Why Wanting to Look Successful Doesn't Always Lead to Success." *Organizational Dynamics*, Fall 2001, 162–171.

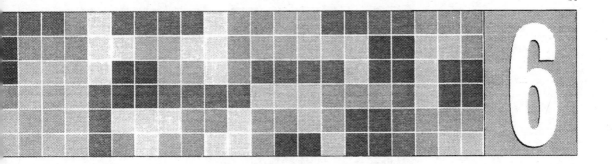

Monitoring Performance

PERFORMANCE GOALS

After studying this chapter and doing the exercises, you should be able to:

- understand that performance stems from factors related to the individual, the manager, the job, and the organization.

- set performance standards and measure performance against these standards.

- take one of three actions after measuring performance: do nothing, solve the problem, or revise the standard.

"Allow me to explain how this company is a better place because of all that I have achieved this year."

UNDERSTANDING PERFORMANCE

Performance is one of the most widely used terms in the workplace. Similar to the word *weather*, the word performance is used so frequently few people ever stop to think of what the term really means. In fact, we searched 10 management textbooks, and not one defined *performance*, despite lengthy discussions of the topic. As used here, **performance** refers to the accomplishment of a work assignment. Performance is not the same as *productivity*, which refers to how many resources are utilized in comparison to the amount of work accomplished. If a worker takes one hour to send a postcard to a customer, the worker has performed the task, but not productively. Because of low productivity, the worker has performed poorly.

Performance stems from, or is caused by, four groups of factors.

1. *Factors related to the individual.* Factors such as attitude, motivation, problem-solving ability, and conscientiousness all influence the level of individual performance. All things being equal, a person with the "right stuff" will perform better.

2. *Factors related to the manager.* A manager who acts as an effective coach will bring about better performance than a manager who does

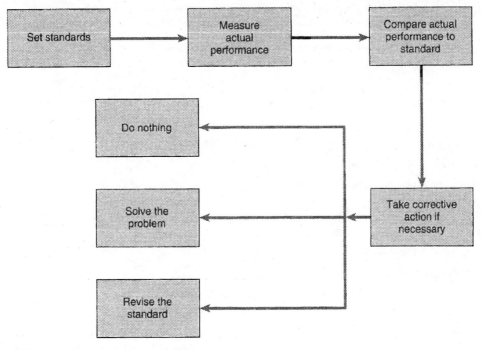

EXHIBIT 6.1   Steps in the monitoring process.

a poor job of coaching. Among the managerial factors enhancing performance are effective communication about job responsibilities, sufficient feedback about job performance, and employee encouragement.

3. *Factors related to the job.* For people to perform well, they need the right equipment and technology. A bright, cheerful work environment without excessive noise is also helpful. Physical demands, including travel, should be reasonable.

4. *Factors related to the organization.* For performance to be high, the organizational culture should encourage good performance. The work-group should also incorporate a norm of high performance. Rewards for high performance also contribute to good performance (see Chapter 8).

The rest of the information about monitoring performance is organized around the diagram in Exhibit 6.1, the basic steps in the monitoring (or controlling) process. You are invited to take the Are You Ready? quiz to reflect on your attitudes toward performance evaluation.

To think through your natural tendencies toward measuring the performance of others, respond to items on the following checklist.

	Generally True	Generally False
1. All workers should be held to tight performance standards.	☐	☐
2. You can measure accurately only the work performed by people who achieve quantitative results such as output per hour.	☐	☐
3. Whatever exists can be measured.	☐	☐
4. Having my performance evaluated is about as much fun as having a bunion removed.	☐	☐
5. I think the president of the United States should receive a thorough performance evaluation by members of Congress each year.	☐	☐
6. I think that employees should contribute to the performance evaluation of company executives.	☐	☐
7. I prepare carefully for my performance evaluation.	☐	☐
8. When I received (or if I received) a low grade in a course, my attitude toward the instructor was (or would be) "So who are you to judge me?"	☐	☐
9. Performance appraisals do not fit modern, team-based and democratic organizations.	☐	☐
10. When I finish reading this book and doing the exercises, I think I just might evaluate how good or poor a job the author did.	☐	☐

Interpretation: If you tend to believe in the value of measuring performance you would answer as follows: 1.Generally True; 2. Generally False; 3. Generally True; 4. Generally False; 5. Generally True; 6. Generally True; 7. Generally True; 8. Generally False; 9. Generally False; 10. Generally True.

You have a positive attitude to employee evaluation if you scored 8, 9, or 10. If you scored 10, you might enjoy controlling others too much. You have average attitudes about evaluating employees if you scored, 5, 6, or 7. You have below average opinions about the contribution of performance evaluation if you scored, 1, 2, 3, or 4.

CRS Objectives	Distinguished Performance (4 points)	Above-Standard Performance (3 points)	Standard Performance (2 points)	Below-Standard Performance (1 Point)
Customer satisfaction	89% or higher overall customer satisfaction	86%–88% overall customer satisfaction	83%–85% overall customer satisfaction	<83% overall customer satisfaction
Calls answered within 30 seconds	Group consistently answers 80% or more of calls within 30 seconds.	Group consistently answers 75%–79% of calls within 30 seconds.	Group consistently answers 70%–74% of calls within 30 seconds.	Group consistently answers <70% of calls within 30 seconds.

EXHIBIT 6.2   Two performance standards for a customer service group.

SETTING STANDARDS TO ACHIEVE PERFORMANCE

Monitoring or controlling performance begins with a set of performance standards that are realistic and acceptable to the people involved. A **standard** is a unit of measurement used to evaluate results. It is difficult to coach group members if you do not have a clear fix in mind about what constitutes acceptable performance. Standards can be quantitative, such as cost of sales, profits, or time to complete an activity. Standards can also be qualitative, such as customer reaction to a landscaping job performed by a landscaping technician. Exhibit 6.2 presents two sets of performance standards established for a customer service representative unit within a telecommunications company.

Historical information about comparable situations will often help provide you the basis for setting initial standards. Assume that as a mortgage officer, you wish to establish a standard for the maximum percentage of delinquent loans. If the delinquency rate for comparable loans in your area has been 1.5 percent, the new standard might be a delinquency rate of no greater than 1.5 percent.

At times, profit-and-loss considerations dictate performance standards. A case in point is the occupancy rate for an office building. Assume that financial analysis reveals that the average occupancy rate must be 80 percent for the building to cover costs. As the building manager, you must then set an occupancy rate of at least 80 percent as a standard.

Employee input about standards should be welcome, for the employee may have excellent ideas about what constitutes success in his or her job.

ACTIVATE YOUR SKILLS: Establishing Performance Standards

Establish a clear set (one, two, or three) of performance standards for the following occupations, or responsibility within an occupation:

1. A firefighter.
2. A customer service representative for a software company call center.
3. The director of a nursing home.
4. The coaching aspect of a manager's position.

An assistant manager in an auto-repair chain shop that specializes in exhaust system replacement added this standard, "I ask that we inspect the customer's brakes while the car is on the rack. We could pick up an enormous amount of business this way."

Employee input should be encouraged at all stages of the evaluation process. Employees should contribute their perceptions of how well they performed. Differences in perception between the supervisor and the employee present lively material for dialogue.

MEASURING ACTUAL PERFORMANCE

To implement the monitoring system, performance must be measured. Performance appraisals are one of the major ways of measuring performance. Supervisors often make direct observations of performance to implement a control system. A simple example would be observing to ensure that a sales associate always asks a customer, "Is there anything else I could show you now?" A more elaborate performance measure would be a 10-page report on the status of a major project submitted to top-level management.

Performance can often be measured by using objective information supplied by the information system. Among these objective measures could be number of sales minus returns, number of accidents, percentage of delinquent loans, the graduation rate of team members for a college coach, or the amount of funds raised by a fund-raiser. The customer service ratings in Exhibit 6.2 may appear to be objective and quantitative. However, they are based on the subjective impressions of customers who rate the extent of their satisfaction.

Performance measurement is much more complex than it would seem on the surface. The following list presents three important conditions for effective performance measurement:[1]

1. *Agree on the specific aspects of performance to be measured.* Top-level managers in a hotel chain might think that occupancy rate is the best meas-

ure of performance. Middle managers might disagree by saying, "Don't place so much emphasis on occupancy rate. If we try to give good customer service, the occupancy rate will take care of itself. Therefore, let's try to measure customer service."

2. *Agree on the accuracy of the measurement needed.* In some instances, precise measurement of performance is possible. Sales volume, for example, can be measured in terms of customer billing and accounts paid. In other instances, precise measurement of performance may not be possible. Assume that top-level managers of the hotel chain buy the idea of measuring customer service. Quantitative measures of customer satisfaction—including the ratings that guests submit on questionnaires and the number of formal complaints—are available. However, many measures would have to be subjective, such as the observation of the behavior of guests, including their spontaneous comments about service.

3. *Agree on who will use the measurements.* In most firms, managers at higher levels have the authority to review performance measures of people below their organizational level. Few people at lower levels object to this practice. A controversial issue that surfaces from time to time is whether teammates should be made aware of each other's performance. You should settle this issue ahead of time.

COMPARING ACTUAL PERFORMANCE TO STANDARDS

After establishing standard and taking performance measurements, you have to move on to the next step of actually comparing performance to standards. Key aspects of comparing performance to standards include measuring the deviation and communication information about it.

Deviation in a monitoring system indicates the size of the discrepancy between performance standards and actual results. It is important to agree beforehand how much deviation from standard is a basis for corrective action. Recall the 80 percent occupancy rate standard in the office building example. A deviation of plus or minus 3 percent may not be considered meaningful but rather caused by random events. Deviations of 4 percent or more, however, would be considered significant.

Sometimes a deviation as small as 1 percent from standard can have a big impact on company welfare, thereby triggering the need for coaching. For example, if a division fails by 1 percent to reach $100 million in sales, the firm has $1 million less money than anticipated. At other times, deviations as high as 10 percent might not be significant. For example, a claims department might be 10 percent behind schedule in processing insurance claims. However, the claims manager might not be upset, knowing that all the claims will be processed eventually.

When statistical limits are not available, it takes wisdom and experience to diagnose a random deviation. Sometimes factors beyond a person's influence lead to a one-time deviation from performance. In such a case, the manager or coach might ignore the deviation. For example, a person might run in poor performance one month because he or she faced a family crisis.

For the monitoring system to work, the results of the comparison between actual performance and standards must be communicated to the person being coached. The feedback should ideally take place soon after you obtain the information from the control system. At a minimum, the feedback should be provided during the performance appraisal. If the employee has met standards, he or she should receive recognition and encouragement.

TAKING CORRECTIVE ACTION

An evaluation of the discrepancy between actual performance and a standard presents a manager/coach with three courses of action: do nothing, solve the problem, or revise the standard. Each of these alternatives may be appropriate, depending on the results of the evaluation.

1. Do Nothing

The purpose of the monitoring system is to determine whether the plans are working. No corrective action is required if the evaluation reveals that events are proceeding according to plan. Nevertheless, an effective coaching technique is to compliment the workers who have met or exceeded standard.

2. Solve the Problem

The big payoff from the controlling and monitoring process concerns the corrections of deviation from substandard performance. If the manager decided that a deviation is significant (nonrandom), he or she starts problem solving. Typically you, as the coach, would meet with the group member to discuss the nature of the problem. In the office building occupancy rate problem, a discussion might reveal that the building manager needs a bigger advertising budget. At other times, a discussion might reveal that the group member who did not meet standard needs to develop the appropriate skills to get the job done. Put on your coaching hat to help the employee improve.

3. Revise the Standard

Deviations from standard are sometimes attributable to errors in planning rather than to performance problems. Corrective action is thus not warranted because the true problem is an unrealistic performance standard. For example, in the months following the September 11, 2001, crisis, the occupancy standard for the Empire State Building had to be lowered. It was no longer realistic to expect to have a waiting list for office space in such a tall and well-known building.

Think It Through   "Who Said I'm Not Performing Well?"

Maria Lopez is the founder and owner of Pleasure Travel, a travel agency located in a suburban mall. Pleasure Travel has four full-time travel agents in addition to Maria, as well as three part-time agents. Up to three years ago, Pleasure Travel had eight full-time agents and five part-timers.

The decrease in the number of agents reflects the decrease in business volume at Pleasure Travel. To help fortify the business, last year Maria bought the customer list from a competitor who was forced out of business due to decreased business and declining profit margins.

Maria attributes the decline in her business to problems that have plagued the industry in recent years. She notes, "Bit by bit the airlines have put the squeeze on us. First they lowered the commissions they pay us. Then a few major carriers stopped paying commissions entirely, which was a dagger in our heart. Another real problem is that many of our former customers are now making travel arrangements over the Internet. Even though it may not always be true, a lot of people believe they can get a better deal by making travel arrangements over the Internet.

"As our commissions from airlines declined or evaporated and our customer base decreased, we had to charge higher fees for our service. As a result, we drove away more customers."

Maria decided that she would try another approach to bolster the sagging fortune at Pleasure Travel. She would establish standards of business volume for her agents, both full-time and part-time. Maria thought, "If I raise the standards 15 percent over the average volume we are achieving now, our commissions from hotels, car rental agencies, and the few airlines that still grant commissions will enable the agency to make a decent profit. Also, the agents will be taking home about a 15 percent increase in their own commissions. It seems like a win-win situation to me."

Maria sent an email message to all staff members about the new performance standards. She also established a before-business-hours meeting to discuss the new standards. Maria began by explaining that for agents to earn a full commission on all their bookings, they would now have to produce 15 percent more business.

The tone of the meeting became somber immediately. Tony Antonelli, one of the veteran agents, said, "Maria, I've been in this business a long time. I particularly like the travel business because I use a wheelchair, and I can conduct my work from one location. Asking us to increase our performance 15 percent to gain our rightful commissions pushes us into a corner. In this business, you can't pull people in off the streets and make them buy airplane tickets. We all know that the fear of flying is worse than it has ever been."

Continued

Naomi Weiss, a part-time agent and relative newcomer to the travel business, expressed another concern: "Maria, with all due respect, please show us the hat from which you pulled the 15 percent figure. Do you think we sit here turning away business so we can surf the Net or play computer games? Your new standards are a tad unrealistic."

Maria then said to the group, "I hear you, but we are slowly going out of business. We need the 15 percent increase to stay profitable."

Questions

1. How justified is Maria in establishing the new performance standards?
2. What steps might have Maria taken to gain better acceptance of her new performance standards?
3. What errors in using the steps in the monitoring process might Maria have made?

Summary

Performance refers to accomplishing a work assignment, and stems from, or is caused by, factors related to the (1) individual, (2) manager, (3) job, and (4) organization. The steps in the monitoring (or controlling) process are (1) set standards, (2) measure actual performance, (3) compare actual performance to standard, and (4) take corrective action. Taking corrective action consists of three alternatives: do nothing, solve the problem, or revise the standard.

Key Terms and Concepts

Deviation   Standard
Performance

Expand Your View

Skill-Building Exercise: Developing Performance Standards

Now that you have been thinking through performance standards, it will prove worthwhile to develop a set of them. Begin with the job you have now or the last job you held if you are not working currently. List the five most important performance standards for your position. For example, a performance standard for a travel agent might be, "Arranges overseas airplane trips for clients at a price and convenience that adds value beyond what the client would ordinarily find by using the Internet."

Next, interview a coworker, friend, or family member to develop a list of five performance standards for his or her job. Ask penetrating questions such as,

"What does your company really expect of you?"

"How will you know when you have done a good job?"

"Describe a make-or-break factor within your job."

After you have completed this assignment, make an entry in your Coaching and Mentoring Diary about what you have learned. For example: How easy is it to specify performance standards?

Questions

1. Why is it important to set both objective and subjective performance standards for professional-level employees?
2. Why do so many employees object to having their performance measured?
3. For what type of work might meeting standard 100 percent of the time be required?
4. Should employees be allowed to set their own performance standards? Explain your reasoning.
5. Suppose a mentor believes that a performance standard (set by the company) for one of his or her protégés is unrealistically high. What advice should the mentor give that person about meeting standard?
6. Describe the most difficult performance standard you have faced. What made it difficult to achieve?
7. How might a parent use the steps in the controlling process to assist in child rearing?

Notes

1. Richard O. Mason and Burton Swanson, "Measurement for Management Decision: A Perspective," *California Management Review* (Spring 1979), 70–81.

Learning Links

Fandray, Dayton. "The New Thinking in Performance Appraisals." *Workforce*, May 2001, 36–46.

Grote, Dick. "Performance Appraisal Reappraised." *Harvard Business Review*, January–February 2000, 21.

Joinson, Carla. "Making Sure Employees Measure Up." *HR Magazine*, March 2001, 36–41.

"Performance Appraisal,"www.performance-appraisal.com/intro.htm (accessed December 6, 2003).

Scott, Susanne G., and Walter O. Einstein. "Strategic Performance Appraisal in Team-Based Organizations: One Size Does Not Fit All." *The Academy of Management Executive*, May 2001, 107–116.

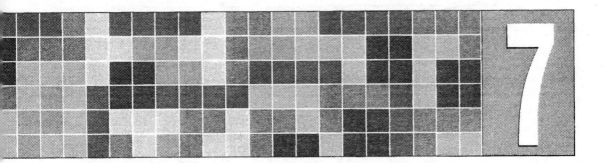

Giving Feedback

PERFORMANCE GOALS

After studying this chapter and doing the exercises, you should be able to:

- explain how feedback can point to developmental opportunities for the person being coached.

- provide effective feedback by watching what you say, giving feedback frequently, and interpreting your observations.

- provide effective feedback by being specific, expressing your feelings, and soliciting feedback on your feedback.

- conduct a productive performance evaluation.

- overcome resistance to feedback by building stronger communication bridges between you and the people being coached or mentored.

"I would like you to give me some feedback on the feedback I gave you. How did you really feel about being ranked 25 out of 25 employees in the department?"

UNDERSTANDING FEEDBACK

Feedback is the information that tells someone how well he or she has performed. As a coach and mentor, giving feedback is a critical part of helping the person you are working with grow professionally and personally. This is how you let your team member or protégé uncover his or her strengths and **developmental opportunities** or weaknesses. Giving feedback helps the person being coached or mentored gain valuable information about himself or herself. Properly done it can help develop self-confidence and direct constructive efforts toward improvement.

Self-concepts are based largely on what others have said about us. This is where your feedback as coach and mentor comes into play. Giving encouraging feedback to the person you are coaching or mentoring can help that person develop a more positive and stronger self-concept. A strong self-concept leads to self-confidence, which has many important implications for job performance. People who are confident are more effective in leadership and sales positions. Self-confident workers are also more likely to set higher goals for themselves and persist in trying to reach their goals.[1]

Few people can sustain a high level of motivation without receiving information about how well they are doing. Even if employees find their work challenging and exciting, they will still need feedback. One reason feedback is valuable is that it acts as a reward. When workers learn that their efforts achieved a worthwhile purpose, they feel encouraged. For example, if a graphics display your protégé designed was well received by company officials, he would probably want to prepare another graphics display.

In the more informal role of coach or mentor, your responsibility is to provide ongoing feedback that is not recorded in the employee's permanent record. As a team leader or supervisor in the coaching role, you may be required to give more formal feedback in the form of a **performance appraisal.** These observations become a permanent part of the employee's personnel record. Whether the feedback is informal or formal, your feedback can affect an employee's salary increase or promotion to another position.

GIVING EFFECTIVE FEEDBACK

Both positive and negative feedback will be better received and have more positive outcomes when you use the following strategies.

1. Watch What You Say

Giving feedback requires building on your empathy skill to find the right words to convey criticism. Most people's egos are too tender to accept the raw truth when faced with disapproval of their thoughts or actions. Translated into action, **diplomacy** often means finding the right phrase to convey disapproval, disagreement, or discontent. Put yourself into their shoes when framing your feedback. Remember that your goal as coach or mentor is to help your team members and protégés to improve, but if you hurt their feelings you will not create the right frame of mind for growth. One method is to begin your feedback by saying something positive before diplomatically stating your criticism.

Among the words and phrases that trigger defensive behavior by the feedback recipient are, "stupid mistake," "laziness," "worst in the department," and "absurd approach to solving the problem." The thought of being the worst is a direct blow to a person's self-esteem.

Being aware of your language when you are giving feedback can also help get your point across more effectively. When instructing somebody else to improve, tell the person he or she *could* do something rather than *should* do it. *Should* implies the person is doing something morally wrong, such as "You should recycle the used-up laser cartridges." *Could* leaves the person with a choice to make: to accept or reject your input and weigh the consequences.[2]

Respond to items on the following checklist to think through your natural tendencies toward giving effective feedback.

	Generally True	Generally False
1. I enjoy making constructive suggestions.	☐	☐
2. I get a kick out of insulting people.	☐	☐
3. I'm pretty good at giving compliments that contain an implied insult like, "You're pretty good with people for being a nerd."	☐	☐
4. I become defensive and angry when someone corrects something I have done.	☐	☐
5. At least several times in my life I have been thanked for suggesting how someone could improve.	☐	☐
6. I think it is cruel for students to make negative comments when they evaluate an instructor for a course.	☐	☐
7. I enjoy giving legitimate compliments to others.	☐	☐
8. Supervisors should forget about giving compliments, because your paycheck tells the true story about your performance.	☐	☐
9. Criticizing coworkers during a meeting is fun for me.	☐	☐
10. I enjoy filling out and sending back the customer satisfaction surveys placed in a hotel or restaurant.	☐	☐
11. I feel comfortable telling a friend what he or she is doing that disturbs me.	☐	☐

Interpretation: The answers in the direction of tendencies toward giving effective feedback are as follows: 1. Generally True; 2. Generally False; 3. Generally False; 4. Generally False; 5. Generally True; 6. Generally False; 7. Generally True; 8. Generally False; 9. Generally False; 10. Generally True; 11. Generally True.

You have positive tendencies toward giving effective feedback if you scored 9, 10, or 11. You have average tendencies toward giving effective feedback if you scored 7, or 8. You have below-average tendencies toward giving effective feedback if you scored 1, 2, 3, 4, or 5.

2. Give Frequent Feedback

To be an effective coach, especially in a supervisory role, one of the most important things to remember is to give frequent feedback. Effective coaches constantly inform team members how they can improve and praise them for things done right. These two types of feedback enable the people being coached to take corrective action if needed and reinforce their continuation of favorable activities. To reinforce a statement made earlier in this book, do not wait for the performance appraisal to give feedback. Giving frequent feedback helps reduce surprises during the formal performance evaluation.

3. Interpret Your Observations

To inform team members and persons you mentor how they can improve, you must use your observation and measurement skills (as discussed in Chapter 6, "Monitoring Performance"); then interpret what is happening. An interpretation given by the person doing the coaching is an explanation of why the person being coached is acting in a particular manner. The interpretation is designed to give this person insight into the nature of the problem. For instance, a food service manager might be listening to the problems of a cafeteria manager with regard to cafeteria cleanliness. After a while the food service manager might say, "You're angry and upset with your employees because they don't keep a careful eye on cleanliness. So you avoid dealing with them, and it only makes problems worse." If the manager's diagnosis is correct, an interpretation can be extremely helpful. The active listening skills described in Chapter 3 will help you interpret your observations.

4. Give Specific Feedback

How you give feedback is just as important as making sure you give it. Feedback is more effective when it is specific. Instead of making generalities about an improvement area for another person, pinpoint areas of concern. A generality might be, "You just don't seem as if you're into this job." A specific on the same problem might be, "You neglect to call in on days that you are going to be out ill. In this way, you are letting down the team." Sometimes it can be effective to make a generalization (such as not being "into the job") after you first produce several concrete examples. Closely related to minimizing generalizations is to avoid exaggerating, for example, by saying such things as "You are always letting down the team." Specific feedback is sometimes referred to as **behavioral feedback** because it pinpoints behavior rather than personal characteristics or attitudes. "Neglecting to call in" pinpoints behavior, whereas "not into the job" focuses more on an attitude.

5. Express Your Feelings

When you give feedback, it is also helpful to express your feelings in addition to conveying the facts. For example, "Our defects are up by 12 percent [fact], and I'm quite disappointed about those results [feelings]." Because feelings contribute strongly to comprehension, you will help overcome a potential communication barrier.

6. Solicit Feedback on Your Feedback

Part of giving effective feedback is making sure your message has been received as intended. A good practice is to conclude a meeting with a question such as, "Okay, what have we agreed upon?" Unless feedback of this nature is obtained, you will not know whether your message has been received until the receiver carries out your request. If the request is carried out improperly, or if no action is taken, you will know that the message was received poorly.

It is preferable to ask your team member or protégé for his or her understanding or interpretation of what you said. For example, you might say after giving feedback, "What is your understanding of our agreement?" Additionally, use nonverbal indicators to gauge how well you delivered your message. A blank expression on the receiver's face might indicate no comprehension. A disturbed, agitated expression might mean that the receiver's emotions are blocking the message. In addition to looking for verbal comprehension and emotions when you have given feedback, actively listen for feelings as the person receiving your feedback responds.

Obtaining feedback is important because it results in two-way communication in which people take turns being sender and receiver, thereby having a dialogue. Dialogues take time because they require people to speak more slowly and listen more carefully. The results of having employees engage in dialogue are said to include a deeper sense of community (a feeling of belongingness) and greater trust among employees.[3] You might relate this finding to your own experiences. Do you trust people better when you both exchange ideas and listen to each other?

7. Mirror to Establish Rapport

Establishing rapport is an important coaching and mentoring tactic. A form of nonverbal communication called **mirroring** can be used to establish such rapport. To mirror someone is to subtly imitate that individual. The most successful mirroring technique for establishing rapport is to imitate the breathing pattern of another person. If you adjust your own breathing rate to someone else's, you will soon establish rapport with that person. The purpose of establishing rapport is that it facilitates giving feedback. When rapport is established, people accept both compliments and criticisms more readily.

ACTIVATE YOUR SKILLS: The Mirroring Technique

To practice mirroring, during the next 10 days each class member schedules one mirroring session with an unsuspecting subject. An ideal opportunity would be an upcoming meeting on the job. Another possibility would be to ask a friend if you could practice your interviewing techniques with him or her—but do not mention the mirroring technique. A third possibility would be to sit down with a friend and conduct a social conversation.

While holding an interview or a discussion with the other party, use the mirroring technique. Imitate the person's breathing pattern, rate of speech, hand movements, eye movements, leg movements, or any other noticeable aspect of behavior.

After the mirroring sessions have been conducted, hold a class discussion about the results. Questions include:

1. Did the other person notice the mirroring and comment on the behavior of the person doing the mirroring?
2. Was the rapport enhanced (or hindered) by the mirroring?
3. How many students intend to repeat the mirroring technique in the future?

Mirroring takes practice. It is a subtle technique that requires a moderate skill level. If you mirror (or match) the person you are coaching in a rigid, mechanical way, you will appear to be mocking him or her. And mocking, of course, erects rather than tears down a communication barrier.

FORMALLY APPRAISING PERFORMANCE

Perhaps 50,000 books, articles, and websites have been devoted to conducting performance appraisals. My conclusion about all this information is that performance appraisals are like preparing an income tax return. Almost everyone recognizes their inevitability; most people dislike them; yet those who are expecting a refund (or a positive evaluation) welcome them. Following are six time-tested suggestions that will make conducting the performance evaluation more pleasant and productive and help place you in the role of a coach and mentor. Keep in mind, also, the other suggestions for feedback provided earlier.

1. *Display a helpful and constructive attitude to the person being evaluated.* A helpful and constructive attitude helps reduce defensiveness about the evaluation and thereby improves chances for two-way communication.

2. *Use tell-and-listen, and problem-solving approaches.* Under tell-and-listen, the manager gives the evaluation and then listens to the group member's reaction to the evaluation. In addition, the evaluee is free to discuss any problems. Using the problem-solving approach, managers act as coaches. Much mutual discussion and idea sharing takes place.

3. *Make sure the true evaluation is communicated.* Often people do not hear negative feedback, and evaluators frequently communicate negative feedback in such a manner that the message is softened. Ask for feedback toward the end of the evaluation session. You might ask, for example, "What did we conclude about your performance for this review period?"

4. *Use short-term, specific improvement goals.* Goal setting is critical in all methods of improving the performance. Short-term, specific goals lead to the quickest improvement. An example would be "By October 31 of this year, I would like to see a 25 percent reduction in inventory. Can you commit to this goal?" Longer-term goals have their place also, particularly in strategic planning.

5. *Be willing to help with job problems beyond the evaluee's control.* To make the performance review developmental in nature, display a willingness to help the person succeed. As the manager, for example, you might be in a position to help resolve such problems as inadequate staff support, obsolete equipment, insufficient budget, insufficient authority, or lack of cooperation from other departments.

6. *Avoid year-end surprises.* One reason some people do not like performance appraisals is that the manager waits six months to one year for the review session in order to discuss a particular mistake the employee made. Much better practice is for the manager to give feedback (both negative and positive) along the way.

7. *Give advance notice about the appraisal session.* Short notice of appraisals can be upsetting for many employees. It is therefore better to give about two weeks notice for the appraisal interview. In this way the employee can prepare for the interview, including preparing any documentation of work accomplishments he or she thinks is useful.

8. *End on a positive note.* Age-old practice suggests ending any evaluation interview on a positive note, even in situations wherein the overall evaluation has been negative. Point out what the employee is doing right and express appreciation for those accomplishments. For instance, the evaluator might say, "We've discussed a few areas for needed improvement, but don't forget that we are pleased with many aspects of your performance. Since you've been in charge of the payroll department, paychecks have not been sent late once to the bank or to employees. And that's very important."

ACTIVATE YOUR SKILLS: Conducting a Preformance Evaluation

You will need a partner to do the role-play described next.

■ *Role of engineering manager.* Today is your day to review the performance of one of your team members—a man with 25 years of design engineering experience. Your evaluation of this team member is generally positive, but you believe strongly that any person can find areas for improvement. You recognize that he does not welcome the review process. You also recognize that it is company policy to review the performance of every employee. In addition, your evaluation must be communicated in person to each person reporting to you.

■ *Role of design engineer.* You believe quite strongly that having your performance evaluated and reviewed is beneath your dignity. Adding to your concern is that you perceive your boss as more of an administrator than an engineer. You know that he has an engineering background, but you consider him to be no longer a professional engineer.

Act out the performance review as it probably would happen. If you are the manager, try to make use of some of the suggestions for providing feedback and evaluating performance made in this and the previous chapter (Chapter 6, "Monitoring Performance").

OVERCOMING RESISTANCE TO FEEDBACK

Any kind of communication is subject to roadblocks and barriers. Giving feedback about someone can be even more charged because the person receiving it may feel he or she is being judged. The following techniques are helpful in building stronger communication bridges between you and the people you coach or mentor.

1. Appeal to Human Needs and Time Your Feedback

People are more receptive to messages that promise to do something for them. In other words, if a message promises to satisfy a need that is less than fully satisfied, you are likely to listen. The person in search of additional money who ordinarily does not hear low tones readily hears the whispered message, "How would you like to earn $400 in one weekend?"

Properly timing your feedback is related to appealing to human needs. It is important to take into account the person's mental condition at the moment. A general principle is to try to give feedback when your team member or protégé is in the right frame of mind to listen. The right frame of mind includes such factors as not being preoccupied with other thoughts, not being frustrated, being in a good mood, and not being stressed out.

2. Repeat by Using More Than One Channel

Repetition, like any other means of overcoming communication roadblocks, does not work for all people. Many people who repeatedly hear the message "drinking and driving do not mix" are not moved by it. Straight repetition can also be annoying.

If you feel your feedback has not been understood or accepted, repeating the message in a different form or using another communication channel is generally effective. For example, follow up a face-to-face discussion with an email message, a telephone call, or both. Your body can be another channel or medium to help impart your message. If you agree with someone about a spoken message, state your agreement and also shake hands over the agreement.

3. Have an Empowered Attitude

According to Sharon Lund O'Neil, a person's communication effectiveness is directly proportional to his or her attitude. The point is that a positive attitude helps a person communicate better in speaking or writing, or nonverbally. **Empowerment** is involved here because the person takes charge of his or her own attitude.[4] Developing a positive attitude is not always easy. A starting point is to see things from a positive perspective, including looking for the good in people and their work. If you see the good in the activities of your team member, you are likely to have a positive attitude. You would then be able to give your feedback with the necessary enthusiasm.

4. Discuss Differences in Paradigms

As mentioned earlier, people often have different frames of reference or paradigms that influence how they interpret events. A **paradigm** is a model, framework, viewpoint, or perspective. When two people look at a situation with different paradigms, a communication problem may occur.

The solution to this communication clash is to discuss the paradigms. Both people live by different rules or guidelines (a major contributor to a paradigm). If the two people can recognize that they are operating within different paradigms, the chances for agreement improve. Keep in mind that people can change their paradigms when the reasons are convincing.[5]

5. Minimize Defensive Communication

People tend to receive feedback in such a way that their self-esteem is protected. This **defensive communication** is also responsible for people sending messages to make themselves look good. For example, when being criticized for low production, an investment banker might blame the advertising agency used by her firm.

Overcoming the barrier of defensive communication requires two steps. First, people have to recognize the existence of defensive communication. Second, they have to try not to be defensive when questioned or criticized. Such behavior is not easy because of the unconscious or semiconscious process of **denial**—the suppression of information we find uncomfortable. For example, the investment banker just cited would find it uncomfortable to think of himself as being responsible for below-average performance.

6. Engage in Small Talk

The term **small talk** has negative connotations for the career-minded person with a professional attitude. Nevertheless, the effective use of small talk and gossip can help a person melt communication barriers. Trainer Randi Fredeig says, "Small talk helps build rapport and eventually trust. It helps people find common ground on which to build conversation."[6] A helpful technique is to collect tidbits of information to use as small talk to facilitate work-related or heavy-topic conversation in personal life. Keeping informed about current events including sports, television, and films provides useful content for small talk.

Think It Through **The Hard-to-Dismiss Purchasing Agent**

Purchasing manager Cora thought to herself, "At last this dreadful incident is coming to an end. I suspect that Marvin, our human resources director, has finally granted me clearance to dismiss George. I can't believe that it has taken two years to fire an employee who refuses to turn in a satisfactory day's work."

Later that day, Cora was perplexed to learn that Jeff, the company CEO, would be joining Cora and Marvin in their discussion about George. Marvin began the meeting:

Cora, might you summarize your argument as to why you are recommending that we fire George, an employee who has been with us for ten years? Jeff would like to hear it directly from you."

As Marvin may have explained, George is incompetent. He won't upgrade himself. He is way behind the curve on e-purchasing. He spends an unreasonable amount of time being entertained by sales representatives. He prefers to avoid purchasing by the Internet whenever

Continued

possible. He often ignores product specifications submitted by other departments. He is clearly the most ineffective purchasing agent in my department. Look at his performance appraisal. I have given George a rating of 'Does not meet minimum requirements of the job' for two consecutive years. Isn't that proof enough?"

"Absolutely not," answered Jeff. "For the previous eight years he received satisfactory or better performance ratings. We cannot dismiss an employee who was a valuable contributor for so many years. You mean to say George's past managers were blind to his faults?"

"I'm not responsible for past ratings. All I know is that I tried coaching George. I've sent him to courses. I praise whatever he does right. My documentation on him must be one inch high and occupy almost an entire floppy disk."

"Nevertheless, we cannot dismiss an employee who gave us eight years of good service. Marvin and I think you should work further with George. We don't want to set a precedent of firing our long-service employees because of a few poor performance appraisals."

Questions

1. What should Cora do next?

2. What do you think of Jeff's (the CEO) policy about not dismissing employees who received high performance evaluations in the past?

3. What comments do you have about the company performance evaluation system?

Summary

Giving feedback is an essential skill in coaching and mentoring. It enables you to help the people being coached or mentored by providing valuable information about themselves, leading them to build a more positive self-concept, and serving as a form of motivation.

Techniques for giving effective feedback include (1) watching what you say, (2) giving frequent feedback, (3) interpreting your observations, (4) giving specific feedback, (5) expressing your feelings, (6) soliciting feedback on your feedback, and (7) mirroring to establish rapport.

Suggestions for conducting a pleasant and productive performance appraisal include (1) be helpful and constructive, (2) use tell-and-listen and problem-solving approaches, (3) make sure the true evaluation is communicated, (4) use short-term, specific improvement goals, (5) help with job problems, (6) avoid year-end surprises, (7) give advance notice, and (8) end on a positive note.

Sometimes a coach or mentor can encounter resistance to needed feedback. In those cases such communication techniques as (1) appealing to human needs and timing your feedback, (2) repeating by using more than one channel, (3) having an empowered attitude, (4) discussing differences in paradigms, (5) minimizing defensive communication, and (6) engaging in small talk can all help build bridges between the coach or mentor and the person he or she is coaching or mentoring.

Key Terms and Concepts

Behavioral feedback

Defensive communication

Denial

Developmental opportunities

Diplomacy

Empowerment

Mirroring

Paradigm

Performance appraisal

Self-concept

Small talk

Expand Your View

Skill-Building Exercise: Feedback in Natural Settings

Giving effective feedback is a complex skill that does not come easily to most people. Guided practice is therefore helpful in developing feedback skills. Look for three opportunities this week to give feedback to someone about his or her interaction with you. When you give the feedback, implement several of the suggestions presented in the chapter section, "Giving Effective Feedback." The feedback might be brief, even taking only about one minute. Here are a few suggestions of persons to whom you might give feedback in natural settings:

1. The technical support person who advises you either in person or by telephone.
2. The store associate who you asked for help or advice.
3. Your dentist, doctor, nurse, lawyer, or paralegal.
4. A family member or friend whose assistance you requested on a problem.

How effective was your feedback? How well did the person or persons respond to positive feedback? What kind of reception did you get with negative feedback. In your Coaching and Mentoring Diary jot down what you learned about your feedback skills.

Questions

1. How does a person know if the feedback he or she receives from another person is accurate?

2. What, if any, ethical problems are involved with mirroring?

3. Suppose a group member has a personal hygiene problem such as bad breath or insufficient showering or bathing. Should the supervisor give feedback about these aspects of behavior?

4. Several management writers have proposed that frequent feedback replace a formal system of performance appraisals. What is your opinion of the value of this suggestion?

5. Suppose your manager does not listen to your suggestions for job improvement. Explain this problem as a paradigm clash.

6. What type of negative feedback has upset you the most? Why do you think you were disturbed by the feedback?

7. What might be a disadvantage to a manager giving all feedback on performance and behavior by email?

Notes

1. Marilyn E. Gist, "Self-Efficacy: Implications for Organizational Behavior and Human Resource Management," *Academy of Management Review* (July 1987), 472–485.

2. "Coach with 'Could,' not 'Should,'" *Executive Strategies* (April 1998), 1.

3. Mark Henricks, "Can We Talk? Speaking Up About the Value of Dialogue," *Entrepreneur* (January 1998),w 82.

4. Sharon Lund O'Neill, "An Empowered Attitude Can Enhance Communication Skills," *Business Education Forum* (April 1998), 28–30.

5. Suzette Haden Elgin, *Genderspeak* (New York: Wiley, 1993).

6. Cited in Jacquelyn Lynn, "Small Talk, Big Results," *Entrepreneur* (August 1999), 30.

Learning Links

Buron, Raoul J., and Dana McDonald-Mann. *Giving Feedback to Subordinates.* Greensboro, NC: Center for Creative Leadership, 1999.

Collins, Michelle LeDuff. *The Thin Book of 360 Feedback: A Manager's Guide.* Plano, TX: Thin Book, 2000.

Johnson, Carla. "Employee Sculpt Thyself. . . with a Little Help." *HR Magazine,* May 2001, 60–64.

Kiger, Patrick J. "Frequent Employee Feedback Is Worth the Cost and Time." *Workforce,* March 2001, 62–65.

Encouraging
Positive Actions

PERFORMANCE GOALS

After studying this chapter and doing the exercises, you should be able to:

- use recognition to reward others.

- motivate others by using compliments effectively.

- encourage continous improvement by using a systematic approach to positive reinforcement.

UNDERSTANDING ENCOURAGEMENT

In coaching and mentoring, one of the most important skills you can develop to help the people you work with is to encourage the positive actions they take toward improving their work behavior. This can best be done through the **behavior modification** strategy of positive reinforcement. When we encourage positive actions, we are motivating a person to engage in constructive behavior.

Positive reinforcement means increasing the probability that behavior will be repeated by rewarding people for making the desired response. The phrase *increasing the probability* means that positive reinforcement improves learning and motivation but is not 100 percent effective. The phrase *making the desired response* is also noteworthy. To use positive reinforcement properly, a reward must be connected to doing something right. Simply paying somebody a compliment or giving the person something of value is not positive reinforcement. Actually modifying behavior involves linking consequences to what the person has or has not accomplished.

Positive reinforcement can be used to encourage desired behaviors that produce profitable products with well-structured jobs, such as data entry or producing parts, and with highly paid, complex jobs, such as scientific research, engineering, and technical development.

Motivating others by giving them **recognition** and **praise** can be considered a direct application of positive reinforcement. Recognition is a strong motivator because it is a normal human need to crave recognition.

The need for recognition is so pervasive that many companies have formal recognition programs to reward outstanding or longtime employees.

Recognition is also effective because most workers feel they do not receive enough. In fact, most people think they are underappreciated (and overworked). Business school dean Gerald Graham found that out of 1,500 workers surveyed, more than 50 percent indicated they seldom or never received oral or written thanks for their efforts.[1] Several studies conducted over a 50-year time span have indicated that employees welcome praise for a job well done as much as a regular paycheck. This finding should not be interpreted to mean that praise is an adequate substitute for salary. Employees tend to regard compensation as an entitlement, whereas recognition is perceived as a gift.[2] Workers, including your coworkers, want to know that their output is useful to somebody.

An outstanding advantage of recognition, including praise, as a motivator, is that it is no cost or low cost, yet powerful. Recognition thus provides an enormous return on investment in comparison to a cash bonus. A challenge in using recognition effectively is that not everyone responds well to the same form of recognition. A good example is that highly technical people tend not to like general praise such as "great job" or "awesome." Instead, they prefer a laid-back, factual statement of how their output made a contribution.

REWARDING POSITIVE ACTIONS

You can encourage growth in your team member's or protégé's development by rewarding their positive actions.

1. Recognize to Reward

The basics of recognition to encourage, motivate, and help those you coach or mentor grow and develop are simple: identify a meritorious behavior and then recognize that behavior with an oral, written, or material **reward.** A list of suitable rewards is given in Exhibit 8.1. Some specific examples of using recognition to encourage desired behavior follow:

- A coworker shows you how to do an important routine you were struggling with on the Internet. Three days later, you send her an email message with a copy to the boss: "Hi Jessica, Your suggestion about copying company logos was dynamite. I've used it five times with success since you showed me what to do." (You are reinforcing Jessica's helpful and cooperative behavior.)
- As the team leader, you receive a glowing letter from a customer about how Kent, one of your team members, solved their problem. You have the letter laminated and present it as a gift to Kent. (The behavior you are reinforcing is good customer service.)

Instructions: Describe how often you act or think in the way indicated by the following statements when you are attempting to motivate another person. Circle the appropriate number for each statement. Scale: very infrequently (VI); infrequently (I); sometimes (S); frequently (F); very frequently (VF).

	VI	I	S	F	VF
1. I ask the other person what he or she is hoping to achieve in the situation.	1	2	3	4	5
2. I attempt to figure out whether the person has the ability to do what I need done.	1	2	3	4	5
3. When another person is heel-dragging, it usually means he or she is lazy.	5	4	3	2	1
4. I explain exactly what I want to the person I'm trying to motivate.	1	2	3	4	5
5. I like to give the other person a reward up front so he or she will be motivated.	5	4	3	2	1
6. I give lots of feedback when another person is performing a task for me.	1	2	3	4	5
7. I like to belittle another person enough so that he or she will be intimidated into doing what I need done.	5	4	3	2	1
8. I make sure that the other person feels treated fairly.	1	2	3	4	5
9. I figure that if I smile nicely I can get the other person to work as hard as I need.	5	4	3	2	1
10. I attempt to get what I need done by instilling fear in the other person.	5	4	3	2	1
11. I specify exactly what needs to be accomplished.	1	2	3	4	5
12. I generously praise people who help me get my work accomplished.	1	2	3	4	5
13. A job well done is its own reward. I therefore keep praise to a minimum.	5	4	3	2	1
14. I make sure I let people know how well they have done in meeting my expectations on a task.	1	2	3	4	5
15. To be fair, I attempt to reward people similarly no matter how well they have performed.	5	4	3	2	1

Continued

16. When somebody doing work for me performs well, I recognize his or her accomplishments promptly.　　1　2　3　4　5

17. Before giving somebody a reward, I attempt to find out what would appeal to that person.　　1　2　3　4　5

18. I make it a policy not to thank somebody for doing a job he or she is paid to do.　　5　4　3　2　1

19. If people do not know how to perform a task, motivation will suffer.　　1　2　3　4　5

20. If properly laid out, many jobs can be self-rewarding.　　1　2　3　4　5

Total Score _____

Scoring and Interpretation: Add the circled numbers to obtain your total score.

90–100　　You have advanced knowledge and skill with respect to motivating others in a work environment. Continue to build on the solid base you have established.

50–89　　You have average knowledge and skill with respect to motivating others. With additional study and experience you will probably develop advanced motivational skills.

20–49　　To effectively motivate others in a work environment you will need to greatly expand your knowledge of motivation theory and techniques.

Sources: The idea for this quiz, and a few items, are from David A. Whetton and Kim S. Cameron, *Developing Management Skills,* 2d ed. (New York: HarperCollins, 1991), pp. 336–337.

■ One member of your department, Jason, is a mechanical engineer. While at a department lunch taking place during National Engineers Week, you stand up and say, "I want to toast Jason in celebration of National Engineers Week. I certainly wouldn't want to be sitting in this office building today if a mechanical engineer hadn't assisted in its construction." (Here the only behavior you are reinforcing is the goodwill of Jason, so your motivational approach is general rather than specific.)

2. Compliment to Motivate

Oral or written recognition may take the form of a **compliment.** Compliments can provide effective encouragement because they make people feel important. Keep in mind that compliments are more likely to encourage people when they are appropriate. *Appropriate* in this context means that

Monetary

Salary increases or bonuses
Company-paid vacation trip
Discount coupons
Company stock
Extra paid vacation days
Bonus or profit sharing
Paid personal holiday (such as birthday)
Movie, concert, or athletic event tickets
Free or discount airline tickets
Discounts on company products or
 services
Gift selection from catalog
Race-car driving camp

Job and Career Related

Challenging work assignment
Empowerment of employee
Change of job status from temporary to
 permanent
Promise of job security
Assignment to high-prestige team or
 project
Favorable performance appraisal
Freedom to choose own work activity
Promotion
Having fun built into work
More of preferred task
Role as supervisor's stand-in when he or
 she is away
Opportunity to contribute to
 presentations to top management
Job rotation
Encouragement of learning and
 continuous improvement
Ample encouragement
Privilege of setting own starting time

Food and Dining

Business luncheon paid by company
Company picnics
Department parties or special banquet
Holiday turkeys and fruit baskets

Recognition and Pride Related

Compliments
Encouragement
Comradeship with boss
Access to confidential information
Pat on back or handshake
Public expression of appreciation
Meeting of appreciation with executive
Flattering letter from customer distributed
 over email
Note of thanks to individual
Open note of thanks distributed over email
Employee-of-the-month award
Wall plaque indicating accomplishment
Special commendation
Company recognition program
Team uniforms, hats, T-shirts, or mugs

Status Symbols

Bigger desk
Bigger office or cubicle
Exclusive use of fax machine or copier
Freedom to personalize work area
Private office
Use of company jet

Time Off

Three-day weekend
Company time bank with deposits made
 for unusual effort or success
Personal leave days for events chosen
 by employee

EXHIBIT 8.1 Rewards suitable for use in positive reinforcement.

Source: A few of the rewards listed here are suggested by Dot Yandle, "Rewarding Good Work: What Do Your Employees Want?" *Success Workshop* (a supplement to *Managers Edge*), May 1999, 1–1; Bob Nelson, "Does One Reward Fit All?" *Workforce,* February 1997, 70; Jennifer J. Laabs, "Targeted Rewards Jump-start Motivation," *Workforce,* February 1998, 88–93; and "Simple Rewards are Powerful Motivations," *HR focus,* August 2001, pp. 10–11.

the compliment fits the accomplishment. Praise that is too lavish may be interpreted as belittling and patronizing.

Let's look at the difference between an appropriate and an exaggerated compliment. Here's the scenario: An executive assistant gets a fax machine operating that was temporarily not sending messages.

- *Appropriate compliment:* "Nice job, Stephanie. Fixing the fax machine took considerable skill. We can now resume sending important fax messages."
- *Exaggerated compliment:* "Stephanie, I'm overwhelmed. You're a world-class fax machine specialist. Are there no limits to your talents?"

Observe that the appropriate compliment is thoughtful and proportionate to what Stephanie accomplished. The exaggerated compliment is probably wasted because it is way out of proportion to the magnitude of the accomplishment.

ENCOURAGING CONTINUOUS IMPROVEMENT

For a coach/mentor to effectively encourage ongoing employee development and improvement, a systematic approach using positive reinforcement works best.

1. State Clearly What Behavior Will Lead to a Reward

You and your team member or protégé must agree on the nature of good performance or the desired goals. Clarification might take this form: "We need to decrease by 40 percent the number of new credit card customers who have delinquent accounts of 60 days or more." Workers also need to know specifically which types of behavior will be rewarded. Unless workers know precisely what they are trying to accomplish, it will be difficult for them to earn a reward.

2. Choose an Appropriate Reward

An appropriate reward is (1) effective in motivating a given person and (2) feasible from the standpoint of the individual or the company. Coaches and mentors must be sensitive to the individual and the individual's cultural background when choosing an appropriate reward for persons they are mentoring. If one reward does not motivate the person, try another. The importance of choosing the right reward underscores the fact that not all rewards are reinforcers. A reward is something of perceived value by the person giving the reward. However, if the reward does not lead to strengthening a desired response (such as wearing safety goggles), it is not a true reinforcer.[3] Refer again to Exhibit 8.1 for a list of suitable rewards.

3. Supply Ample Feedback

Behavior modification cannot work without frequent **feedback.** Feedback can take the form of simply telling people they have done something right or wrong. Brief email messages or handwritten notes are other forms of feedback. Many effective motivators, including Jack Welch, the former longtime CEO of General Electric, make extensive use of handwritten thank-you notes. (For more techniques, see Chapter 7, "Giving Feedback.")

4. Schedule Rewards Intermittently

Rewards should not be given on every occasion of good performance. **Intermittent rewards** sustain desired behaviors longer and also slow down the process of behaviors fading away when they are not rewarded. If each correct performance results in a reward, the behavior will stop shortly after a performance in which the reward is not received. Another problem is that a reward given continuously may lose its impact. A practical value of intermittent reinforcement is that it saves time. Few managers or team leaders have enough time to dispense rewards for every correct action by group members.

5. Make Sure the Reward Follows the Observed Behavior Closely in Time

For maximum effectiveness, people should be rewarded soon after doing something right. A built-in, or intrinsic, feedback system, such as a computer program working or not working, capitalizes on this principle. If you are administering rewards, strive to administer them the same day they are earned.

6. Make the Reward Fit the Behavior

People who are inexperienced in applying positive reinforcement often overdo the intensity of spoken rewards. When an employee does something of an ordinary nature correctly, simple words of praise such as "good job" are preferable to something like "fantastic performance." A related idea is that the magnitude of the reward should vary with the magnitude of the accomplishment.

7. Make the Rewards Visible

Another important characteristic of an effective reward is its **visibility** to other employees. When other workers notice the reward, its impact multiplies because other people observe what kind of behavior is rewarded.[4] Assume that you are being informed that a coworker received an exciting assignment because of high performance. You might strive to accomplish the same level of performance.

8. Change the Reward Periodically

Rewards do not retain their effectiveness indefinitely. Employees and customers lose interest in striving for a reward they have received many times in the past. This is particularly true of repetitive statements such as "Nice job" or "Congratulations." It is helpful for the person giving out the rewards to study the list of potential rewards and try different ones from time to time.

Think It Through	The Ski and Golf Seasonal Workers

Skiing and golf, two of the best amenities in the Bend, Oregon, region, are not designed just for visitors. Most working-class locals struggle to find the time and the money to fit the costly recreational activities into their daily lives. Mount Bachelor, Inc., which during the ski season hires about 450 employees, and Sunriver Resort, which has 350 jobs to fill each summer, have teamed together to create a year-round recreational industry. Employees receive medical and dental benefits, free skiing and golf, and an opportunity to shift jobs each season.

Although a group within the local workforce already transfers between these two employers each season, the companies are enticing workers to return to their positions each year with added medical benefits. Pat Gerhart, human resources director at Mount Bachelor, says that creating the benefits package is a natural evolution from job fair efforts and active recruitment. Benefits bridge the gap between seasons if the first job is cut short before the next one begins.

Workforce availability shortages have prompted the human resources departments to put their heads together and find a way to bring people back year after year, because once a seasonal employee leaves the area, it's hard to get him or her back," Gerhart says.

Experience Wanted

Both companies would like to benefit from experienced and well-trained employees. Sunriver human resources director Joyce Luckman says the resort hopes to retain its core staffs, who will grow their customer service skills in the reciprocal employment program. "There's a need in Central Oregon for year-round employment, and there's a perfect niche in this partnership."

The program benefits both sides. Although insurance for the employees is an added cost for the business, Luckman and Gerhart say it's worth it. Plus, Luckman adds, the employees won't file for unemployment insurance benefits when their seasons end.

The program will be available to all employees but initially is limited to 25 employees on a first-come, first-served basis because the human resources directors want to keep the program small in its first year. "We want to keep it manageable to see what pitfalls we might run into," says Gerhart, adding that they are still working out details.

Continued

Program Will Grow

Gerhart hopes that eventually there will be no number limits and that anyone who wants can participate. Gerhart says the program will grow to include Eagle Crest employees, the Inn of the Seventh Mountain, and maybe the Riverhouse and rafting companies, too. But employers would have to meet some minimum coverage requirement similar to the packages offered by Sunriver and Mount Bachelor. Benefits kick in when the employees enter their second season, so last summer's Sunriver employees working at the winter resort would now be covered.

Most Jobs Pay Low

Gerhart acknowledges that the majority of resort jobs don't pay family wages. She therefore hopes to see more people on the higher end of the pay scale, like groomers and golf course technicians, take advantage of the program. These workers could make a year-round family wage while bringing their families in on the recreational benefits. Besides a season pass for the whole family, Mount Bachelor employees in the program receive a company-paid medical and dental program worth $185 a month. The major medical program has a $250 deductible and the dental insurance a $25 deductible. Employees also receive 80 percent of most expenses paid and up to $300 worth of preventive care.

Sunriver offers employees in the program a full recreation package, including free golf at Meadows and Woodlands, as well as bike and canoe rentals and other discounts at the resort.

Employees in the reciprocal program receive health insurance for the entire family. The company picks up two-thirds of the premium, which can be worth as much as $450 per family per month.

Managers at Mount Bachelor and Sunriver hope that their initiatives in providing year-around pay and increased employee benefits will help develop a more experienced and stable workforce.

Questions

1. What needs are managers attempting to satisfy with their new program of encouraging workers to stay as employees of the resort?

2. What other steps should managers at the golf resorts and ski resorts take to encourage experienced workers to return?

3. What is your prediction of the success of the new pay and benefits in building a stable workforce by motivating employees to return season after season?

4. Imagine yourself as a seasonal worker in the golf and ski industries. How would you motivate yourself to (1) work year-round, and (2) return for several seasons?

Source: Based on information in Anne Aurand, "Resorts Offer Benefits to Seasonal Employees," Bend: OR, *The Bulletin*, March 11, 2000.

Summary

A skilled coach or mentor can encourage employees to grow and develop through positive reinforcement or by rewarding somebody for doing something right. One powerful application of positive reinforcement is recognition. Recognition involves identifying the positive behavior you want to continue and then rewarding the employee orally, in writing, or materially. Giving appropriate compliments to the positive action is an effective method of recognition.

A systematic approach to encouraging the people you coach or mentor can more effectively sustain positive behaviors. This approach involves the following eight steps: (1) stating clearly what behavior will lead to a reward, (2) choosing an appropriate reward, (3) supplying ample feedback, (4) scheduling rewards intermittently, (5) making sure the reward follows the observed behavior closely in time, (6) making the reward fit the behavior, (7) making the rewards visible, and (8) changing the reward periodically.

Key Terms and Concepts

Behavior modification	Praise
Compliment	Recognition
Feedback	Reward
Intermittent reward	Visibility
Positive reinforcement	

Expand Your View

Skill-Building Exercise: Rewarding a Customer Service Representative

One student plays the role of the person attempting to encourage positive actions of (motivate) the other individual. Another student plays the role of the person who is the recipient of these attempts at encouragement.

The customer service manager carefully reviews customer service reports to discover that one service rep has resolved the most complaints for four weeks in a row. Since this rep has been on the job only six months, the manager wants to make sure the rep feels amply rewarded and appreciated. The manager calls the rep into the office to discuss this outstanding performance and give an appropriate reward.

The most fundamental principle of human motivation is that people are motivated by self-interest. This principle is referred to as "What's in it for me?" or WIIFM (pronounced *wiff'em*). Reflect on your own experience. Before working hard to accomplish a task, you probably want to know how you will benefit. If your manager asks you to work extra hours to take care of an emergency, you will most likely oblige. Yet underneath you might be thinking, *If I work these extra hours, my boss will think highly of me. As a result, I will probably receive a good performance evaluation and maybe a better-than-average salary increase.*

A perplexing issue is how the WIIFM principle explains why people are motivated to help others. Why would a company president donate gift baskets of food to the homeless? Why hire a virtually unemployable person for a non-productive job in the mail room? People who perform acts of social good receive the reward of feeling better about themselves. In psychological terms, they satisfy their needs to nurture (take care of) others. More cynically, helping the unfortunate leads to recognition for being a Good Samaritan.

According to Gerald Kushel, to use the WIIFM principle in motivating others, you have to be aware of the intensity of the person's desire.[5] A person can be highly motivated, mildly motivated, or only slightly motivated, depending on the intensity of his or her WIIFM principle. A company might offer outstanding performers the opportunity to work at home one day per week. Employees who are intensely motivated to work at home will work virtually up to capacity to achieve a rating of outstanding performer.

To use the WIIFM principle in motivating others you must find out what needs, desires, or motives a person is attempting to satisfy. In general language, responding to the needs of people is referred to as *touching their hot buttons*. You find out what these needs are by asking people what they want or by observing what interests them. For instance, the way a manager might motivate a recognition-hungry group member is to tell that person, "If you perform 10 percent above quota for six consecutive months, we will get you a plaque to hang on the wall signifying your achievement."

Employee needs have been classified in many ways, yet most of these lists overlap. According to a representative classification, 99 percent of employees are motivated by one or more of the following seven needs:

1. *The need for achievement.* Employees with strong achievement needs seek the satisfaction of completing projects successfully. They want to apply their talents to attain success and find joy in accomplishment for its own sake.

Continued

2. *The need for power.* Employees with a strong power need derive satisfaction from influencing and controlling others and aspire toward becoming executives. These employees like to lead and persuade and be in charge of resources such as budgets.

3. *The need for affiliation.* Employees with a strong need for affiliation derive satisfaction from interacting with others, being part of a work group, and forming friendships. The same employees are motivated to avoid working alone for long periods of time.

4. *The need for autonomy.* Employees with a strong need for autonomy seek freedom and independence, such as having almost complete responsibility for a project. The same employees are motivated to avoid working in a team effort for long periods of time. Many industrial sales representatives (those who sell to companies) have a strong need for autonomy.

5. *The need for esteem.* Employees with a strong need for esteem want to feel good about themselves, and they judge their worth to a large extent based on how much recognition and praise they receive.

6. *The need for safety and security.* Employees with strong needs for safety and security seek job security, steady income, ample medical and dental insurance, and a hazard-free work environment.

7. *The need for equity.* Employees with a strong need for equity seek fair treatment. They often compare working hours, job responsibilities, salary, and privileges with coworkers' and will become discouraged if coworkers receive better treatment.[6]

Recognizing such needs, as well as other needs and interests, helps you apply the WIIFM principle. This principle is based on behavior modification because it points you toward the most effective reward for encouraging an individual.

Others in the class observe the scenario so they can provide feedback on how well behavior modification principles were applied.

Questions

1. Why is it important to make people feel important?

2. Identify several rewards in Exhibit 8.1 that you think would be particularly effective in motivating managers and professionals. Explain your reasoning.

3. Answer question 2 for entry-level service workers, such as supermarket cashiers.

4. Answer question 2 for *numero uno*. What are your most important motivators?

5. Give an example of an appropriate compliment you might give to a coworker who found some information you vitally needed to complete an important project.

6. Give an example of an exaggerated compliment you might give to a coworker who found some information you vitally needed to complete an important project.

7. What rewards are you anticipating from having mastered the information in this chapter?

Notes

1. Cited in "Motivating Entry-Level Workers: Invest Your Time to Boost Their Morale," *Working Smart*, (October 1998), 2.

2. Jennifer Laabs, "Satisfy Them with More Than Money," *Workforce*, (November 1998), 43.

3. Fred Luthans and Alexander D. Stajkovic, "Reinforce for Performance: The Need to Go Beyond Pay and Even Rewards," *Academy of Management Executive*, (May 1999), 52.

4. Steven Kerr, *Ultimate Rewards: What Really Motivates People to Achieve* (Boston: Harvard Business School Publishing, 1997).

5. Gerald Kushel, *Reaching the Peak Performance Zone: How to Motivate Yourself and Others to Excel* (New York: AMACOM, 1994), 66.

6. Research summarized in "One of These Seven Things Will Motivate Any Employee in the Company," *The Motivational Manager*, (sample issue, 1998) (Lawrence Communication, Inc.).

Learning Links

"Behavior-Based Performance Strategies." www.pmanagement.com/BBPS/BBPS.asp (accessed December 6, 2003).

Clemmer, Jim. "Weak Leaders Try to Use Money as a Motivator." www.clemmer.net/excerpts/weak_leaders.shtml

Frase-Blunt, Martha. "Driving Home Your Awards Program." *HR Magazine*, February 2001, 109–115.

www.nationalbusiness.org/NBAWEB/Newsletter/462.htm

Nelson, Bob. "Long-Distance Recognition." *Workforce*, August 2000, 50–52.

Terez, Tom. "A Tale of Two Motivators." *Workforce*, July 2001, 22–23.

Wilson, Thomas B. *Rewards That Drive High Performance: Success Stories from Leading Organizations.* New York: AMACOM, 1999.

Wiscombe, Janet. "Can Pay for Performance Really Work?" *Workforce*, August 2001, 28–34.

Zingheim, Patricia K., and Jay R. Schuster. *Pay People Right! Breakthrough Reward Strategies to Create Great Companies.* San Francisco: Jossey-Bass, 2000.

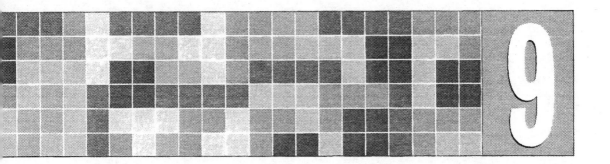

Discouraging Negative Actions

PERFORMANCE GOALS

After studying this chapter and doing the exercises, you should be able to:

* state clearly what behavior leads to punishment and choose an effective punishment.

* supply ample feedback about negative actions and make punishments timely.

* make the punishment fit the behavior.

* make the punishment visible.

"I wonder if I can find a thumb-screw machine on eBay. Top management has started a program of progressive discipline, and I want to have all the necessary equipment."

UNDERSTANDING DISCOURAGEMENT OF NEGATIVE ACTIONS

Success in coaching and mentoring depends a great deal on your skill in encouraging positive action and growth. Positive reinforcement is the most effective strategy you can use as a coach or mentor. Despite the effectiveness of positive motivators, success in coaching and mentoring also requires discouragement of the negative actions of the person being coached or mentored. Coaches and mentors must also address what happens when their team members or protégés do something wrong, do not make necessary improvements, or behave negatively.

For the coach in a supervisory role, this involves using punishment or discipline. **Punishment** is the presentation of an undesirable consequence or the removal of a desirable consequence because of unacceptable behavior. For example, a supervisor can punish an employee by suspending the employee for violating an important safety rule or by taking away her chance to earn overtime pay because of violating the rule.

USING PUNISHMENT

As with encouraging positive actions, a systematic approach to discouraging negative behavior is most effective. You can also intertwine punishment as

Responding to items on the following checklist will help you reflect on your willingness to bring about negative consequences for people whose performance and/or behavior is unacceptable.

	Generally Agree	Generally Disagree
1. Any violation of company policy should lead to an official reprimand.	☐	☐
2. If caught driving while intoxicated, even for the first time, the convicted person should spend a minimum of one week in jail.	☐	☐
3. I would fire an employee if he or she were caught watching a pornographic website on the job.	☐	☐
4. Executives who engage in insider stock trading (profiting from information not available to the public) should be fired and made to pay back any profits from the trade.	☐	☐
5. Taking home a company ballpoint pen for personal use is a crime that should receive an official reprimand.	☐	☐
6. A person caught driving 10 miles per hour past the highway speed limit should lose his driver's license for one year.	☐	☐
7. Being hungry and malnourished does not justify a person stealing food from a large supermarket.	☐	☐
8. College professors should drop a student one grade for each class absence (except for a documented medical emergency).	☐	☐
9. Telling an off-color joke on the job should lead to at least a one-day suspension without pay.	☐	☐
10. If any of the advice in this book backfires, the author should be required to pay me $500.	☐	☐

Interpretation: If you agreed with 8, 9, or 10 of the above statements, you have a strong propensity to punish people. If you agreed with 4, 5, 6, or 7 of the statements, you have an average tendency to be willing to punish people. If you agreed with 1, 2, or 3 of the statements, you prefer to avoid punishing others.

an alternative consequence into many of the steps used in encouraging positive behavior to provide **negative reinforcement,** rewarding people by taking away an uncomfortable consequence of their behavior. (Negative reinforcement, also called avoidance motivation, should not be confused with punishment. In fact, it is the opposite of punishment. It involves rewarding someone by removing a punishment or uncomfortable situation.)

1. State Clearly What Will Lead to a Punishment

Workers need to know specifically which types of behavior will lead to punishment, such as being late for work three or more times in one month. Unless workers know precisely what they are trying to avoid, it will be difficult for them to avoid being punished.

2. Choose an Appropriate Punishment

When rewards do not work, punishment may be necessary. It is generally best to use the mildest form of punishment that will motivate the person, such as simply giving the person negative feedback. Here is a list of potential punishments:

On-the-Job Potential Punishments

Feedback on undesired behavior

Documentation of poor performance

Criticism

Withdrawal of privileges

Undesirable assignment, including being assigned the worst
   equipment in the office

Refusing to cooperate with coworker

Excluding person from group social activities, such as being invited
   to lunch

Reporting on coworker to management

Threat of sanctions

Fining

Withholding of any valued reward

Probation

Suspension

Firing

3. Supply Ample Feedback

As with encouraging positive growth, discouraging negative actions cannot work without frequent feedback to individuals. Feedback can take the form of simply telling people they have done something right or wrong. Negative feedback by email should be written tactfully to avoid resentment. The coach can take advantage of giving face-to-face feedback during formal coaching sessions.

Choose carefully the place or setting for negative feedback. We all know that giving negative feedback in public is uncomfortable for the recipient. With the open work areas in many modern workplaces, finding a quiet, private place for delivering negative feedback becomes more challenging. Delivering negative feedback in a cubicle is acceptable as long as another person is not nearby at the time.

4. Make Sure the Punishments Follow the Observed Behavior Closely in Time

For maximum effectiveness, people should be punished soon after doing something wrong. If you are administering punishments, strive to administer them the same day they are earned.

Punishments delivered more than a week after a violation might be perceived as unjust. The person might think, "I haven't repeated that mistake so I shouldn't be punished now."

5. Make the Punishment Fit the Behavior

The punishment should fit the crime. An employee should not be fired for one small expense account irregularity; an executive guilty of quid pro quo sexual harassment should not receive only a spoken warning.

ACTIVATE YOUR SKILLS: Punishing a Customer Service Representative

One student plays the role of the person attempting to discipline the other individual. Another student plays the role of the person who is the recipient of these attempts at punishment.

The customer service manager carefully reviews customer service reports to discover that one service rep has resolved the fewest complaints for four weeks in a row. Furthermore, three customers have written the company complaining of rude treatment by this same representative. Since this rep has been on the job only six months, the manager wants to make sure the rep begins to make substantial improvements. The manager calls the rep into the office to discuss this poor performance and administer an appropriate punishment.

Others in the class observe the scenario so they can provide feedback on how well punishment steps were applied.

6. Make the Punishments Visible

Most people are aware that public punishments are poor human relations. Yet when coworkers become aware of what behaviors are punished, they receive an important message. A good example took place in a security systems office when a new member of the team distributed a series of sexually offensive jokes by email to coworkers. The man was immediately put on probation, and coworkers received a message about what constitutes unacceptable behavior.

USING EFFECTIVE DISCIPLINE

Punishment on the job is often referred to as **discipline.** However, *discipline* is more closely tied in with company regulations, union regulations, and governmental law. Before administering discipline, it is important to understand company rules on the subject. For example, in your company it might be necessary to have a third-party witness present when administering discipline over a serious matter. To discourage potential lawsuits later, it is important to document in writing all instances of discipline. This is true because if an employee is fired without just cause, he or she might sue the company for unjust firing. A few key concepts about employee discipline follow.

Summary discipline is the immediate discharge of an employee because of a serious (and often illegal) offense. The employee is fired on the spot for rule violations such as stealing, fighting, sexually assaulting another employee, or selling illegal drugs on company premises. In unionized firms, the company and the union have a written agreement specifying which offenses are subject to summary discipline.

Corrective discipline allows employees to correct their behavior before punishment is applied. Employees are told that their behavior is unacceptable and that they must make corrections if they wish to remain with the firm. Corrective discipline incorporates coaching. The manager and the employee share the responsibility for solving the performance problem.

Progressive discipline is the step-by-step application of corrective discipline, proceeding as follows: confrontation, discussion, and coaching → oral warning → written warning → suspension or disciplinary layoff → discharge.

The manager confronts and then coaches the person with poor performance or unacceptable behavior about the problem. If the employee's performance or behavior does not improve, the employee is informed in writing that improvement must be made. The written notice often includes a clear statement of what will happen if performance does not improve. The "or else" could be a disciplinary layoff or suspension. If the notice is ignored and the disciplinary action does not lead to improvement, the employee may be discharged.

Despite its age, progressive discipline is still widely used for two reasons. First, progressive discipline provides the documentation necessary to avoid legal liability for firing poorly performing employees. Second, many labor-management agreements require progressive discipline because of the inherent fairness of the step-by-step procedure.

In a recent development in discipline, the group or team assumes some of the disciplinary activity that was formerly the manager's sole responsibility. Sharing responsibility for discipline reflects the empowerment of teams to carry out managerial functions. The team, for example, might recommend a one-week suspension for one employee who harassed another.[1]

The **red-hot-stove rule** is a time-tested way of administering discipline fairly. According to this rule, employee discipline should be the immediate result of inappropriate behavior, just as a burn is the result of touching a very hot stove. The employee should receive a warning (the red metal), and the punishment should be immediate, consistent, and impersonal. The rules for the effective use of punishment also apply to discipline.

The coach or mentor who cannot officially employ discipline can discourage undesirable behavior through a behavior modification strategy called "extinction." **Extinction** is decreasing the frequency of undesirable behavior by removing the desirable consequence of such behavior. A company might use extinction by ceasing to pay employees for making frivolous cost-saving suggestions. Extinction is sometimes used to eliminate annoying behavior. Assume that a team member persists in telling gross jokes. The joke telling can often be extinguished by the group's agreeing not to laugh at the jokes. Recognize that extinction has limited application on the job because the supervisor/coach/mentor is generally thought to be a person who responds to both positive and negative behavior.

Think It Through   Revenge Has Its Price

Peggy Waterman was the senior secretary to the regional vice president of a financial services firm, a position she held for years. In Peggy's contacts with other regional offices, she discovered that her counterparts were promoted to executive assistants. Peggy wanted to be an executive assistant because the position would give her more status, salary, and vacation time. She approached Ken Jackson, her manager, and requested a promotion to executive assistant.

Ken liked the idea, and asked Peggy to draft a job description that would increase her level of responsibilities, including work on special assignments. Ken reviewed the

Continued

description with Peggy, contacted the headquarters human resource department, and secured the reclassification. Peggy could not understand why Ken was placing more demands on her time and requesting that she accomplish more tasks independently. Ken, in turn, could not understand why Peggy was blocking his requests because it was she who had asked for the promotion.

Peggy would openly complain, "What good is it to be an executive assistant and get more vacation time? Every time I turn around, Ken has some new project for me. I never get to take the vacation time I have." Peggy soon began bad-mouthing Ken. She would answer his telephone calls and say such things as, "I don't know where Ken is. He never tells me anything anymore."

Peggy's disgruntlement continued, and she stopped providing Ken with the information she was supposed to. On one occasion, Peggy scheduled several people to meet with Ken but did not tell him about it until the last minute when a group suddenly appeared at his office. Peg insisted to Ken, "I told you the meeting was scheduled. Don't you listen to me anymore?" Her rhetorical question was asked in front of the guests who had arrived for the meeting.

Peggy insisted that all the information sent to Ken had to be reviewed by her first, and that email messages for Ken be sent to her for forwarding. Even hard-copy items were plucked from Ken's box and reviewed. Peggy would then openly pass judgment on the contents. Once she told a manager reporting to Ken that he would most certainly approve a promotion for one of her people. Yet Ken had not yet read the request.

One day the company CEO telephoned Ken, and Peggy took the opportunity to describe Ken's inability to run his operation. Upon speaking to Ken, the CEO said, "Muzzle her or fire her. I don't care which." Later that day, Ken confronted Peggy: "Ever since your promotion, your performance and attitude have deteriorated. Worse yet, your loyalty to me and the organization has vanished. You wanted a promotion to executive assistant. You wanted all the advantages that go along with the position.

"Two things you didn't take into account. First, in order to attain that level, we expected a higher caliber of work. Not only did you not give us that, your performance deteriorated. Second, your constant harping about my work amounts to insubordination. I am recommending that you be demoted to an entry-level position in the staff support center. After one year of good performance, you may reapply for the position of senior secretary."

Peggy was stunned. She left work for the day to decide on her options.

Questions

1. How just was the punishment Ken administered to Peggy?
2. How might Ken have used corrective discipline in this situation?
3. Where did Ken go wrong in discouraging Peggy's negative actions?

Summary

While positive reinforcement is the most effective strategy for helping people grow and develop, you must also discourage your team member's or protégé's negative actions. Coaches in managerial roles can use punishment or discipline to accomplish this. Although discipline is not usually available to coaches and mentors in nonmanagerial roles, both mentors and coaches can use extinction as a method of discouraging unwanted behavior in the people they work with. Punishment can also be used as an alternative consequence reward in negative reinforcement, which is a strategy for rewarding by taking away the punishment.

As with using positive reinforcement, you will have more success using punishment if it is approached systematically by (1) stating clearly what type of behavior will lead to punishment, (2) choosing an appropriate punishment, (3) supplying ample feedback, (4) making sure the punishments follow the observed behavior closely in time, (5) making the punishment fit the behavior, and (6) making the punishments visible.

Punishment is often referred to as discipline, yet discipline is more closely tied to regulations and law. Summary discipline is the immediate discharge of an employee because of a serious (and often illegal) offense. Corrective discipline allows employees to correct their behavior before punishment is applied; it involves coaching. Progressive discipline is the step-by-step application of corrective discipline, beginning with an oral warning and concluding with discharge as a last resort.

According to the red-hot-stove rule, employee discipline should be the immediate result of inappropriate behavior. The employee should receive a warning, and the punishment should be immediate, consistent, and impersonal.

Key Terms and Concepts

Corrective discipline

Discipline

Extinction

Feedback

Negative reinforcement

Progressive discipline

Punishment

Red-hot-stove rule

Summary discipline

Questions

1. Give an example of an assignment that would be perceived by some employees to be a punishment yet perceived by others to be a reward.

2. Why might punishing an employee by suspending him or her for a day without pay backfire as a punishment?

3. What do you think would be an appropriate punishment for an employee who was running a betting parlor on company computer equipment?

4. Give an example of how you might motivate a high-performing employee by using negative reinforcement.

5. What would be an effective form of punishment for getting you to stop engaging in behavior your employer did not like?

6. What would be an effective form of punishment for an employee who worked for one computer manufacturer, yet brought a laptop made by a competitor to the office each workday?

7. Why is receiving negative feedback often an effective punishment, even when not accompanied by another negative motivator such as a written reprimand?

Notes

1. Robert C. Liden et al., "Management of Poor Performance: A Comparison of Manager, Group Member, and Group Disciplinary Decisions," *Journal of Applied Psychology*, (December 1999), 846.

Learning Links

"Poor Performance: There Is No Negative Consequence to Them for Poor Performance." www.navis.gr/manager/poor_per.htm

Weisinger, Hendrie. *The Power of Positive Criticism.* New York: AMACOM, 2000.

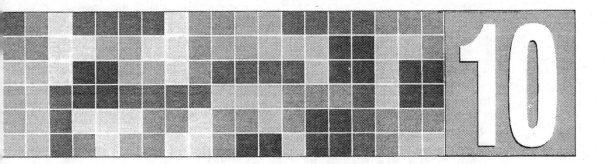

Training Team Members

PERFORMANCE GOALS

After studying this chapter and doing the exercises, you should be able to:

■ enhance learning by encouraging concentration, using motivated interest, and helping the trainee intend to remember.

■ enhance learning by encouraging distributed practice, making the material meaningful, and giving feedback on progress.

■ enhance learning by relying on the magic number seven and encouraging reflection about what is learned.

■ facilitate informal learning through such means as sharing ideas.

"Here's to informal learning."

UNDERSTANDING TRAINING

A direct way of helping others in the workplace is to train them. **Training** is the process of helping others acquire a job-related skill. Supervisors and trainers are responsible for much of the training in organizations. Yet as organizations operate with fewer managers, coworkers have more responsibility to train each other. Therefore, anyone in coaching and mentoring roles needs to be able to effectively train new and current employees. Many successful people give substantial credit to their mentors for having *trained* them properly.

Training is related to other topics studied in this book, especially those in Chapter 6 about monitoring performance and in the section of Chapter 7 about performance appraisals. The content of training programs is influenced by what performance standard the supervisor and higher-level management decide are necessary. If you believe that using correct grammar in speech is a performance standard for customer-service workers, you might have a training program that includes instruction in correct grammar usage in speech.

Performance appraisals are closely linked to training because deficits in performance reveal training needs. For example, if the performance appraisal results for a large number of employees indicate that they are deficient in suggesting imaginative ideas for improving operations or product appeal, the company might sponsor creativity training.

TRAINING EFFECTIVELY

While training others, keep in mind that the following time-tested principles facilitate learning—and therefore training. Applying these principles consistently will increase the chances that the people you are training will acquire new skills. Keep in mind that training is a vast topic. The purpose of this chapter is to provide a few useful suggestions for being an effective trainer.

1. Encourage Concentration

Not much learning takes place unless the trainee concentrates carefully on what is being taught. Concentration improves the ability to do both mental and physical tasks. In short, encourage the person you are training to concentrate.

2. Use Motivated Interest

People learn best when they are interested in the problem facing them. Explain to the trainee how the skill being taught will enhance his or her value as an employee, or relate the skill to the person's professional goals. Trainees can be encouraged to look for some relationship between the information at hand and their personal welfare. With this relationship in mind, the person will have a stronger intention to learn.

3. Intend to Remember

We often do not remember something because we did not intend to commit it to memory. Many executives are particularly effective at remembering names of employees and customers. When one executive was asked how she could commit so many names to memory, she replied, "I look at the person, listen to the name, and try to remember." The next time you travel by car to a sporting event or concert at a large stadium, try to remember where you parked the car, such as saying to yourself, "We parked in section H2." Your

---

ARE YOU READY?   **Attitudes Toward Helping Others**

Directions: Describe how well you agree with the following statements by using a three-point scale: disagree (D); neutral (N); agree (A).

1. If I see a coworker make a mistake, I do not inform him or her of the
   mistake.   D N A

Continued

2. It should be part of everybody's job to share skills and ideas with coworkers. **D N A**

3. The manager should have exclusive responsibility for coaching people within the work unit. **D N A**

4. I can think of many instances in my life when somebody thanked me for showing him or her how to do something. **D N A**

5. I have very little patience with coworkers who do not give me their full cooperation. **D N A**

6. To save time, I will do a task for another person rather than invest the time showing him or her how to do it. **D N A**

7. I would take the initiative to put an inexperienced worker under my wing. **D N A**

8. As a child, I often took the time to show younger children how to do things. **D N A**

9. Rather than ask a coworker for help, I will wait until the manager is available to help me. **D N A**

10. It is best not to share key information with a coworker because that person could then perform as well as or better than me. **D N A**

Score: _____

Scoring: Use the following score key to obtain your score for each answer, and then calculate your total score.

1. D = 3, N = 2, A = 1
2. D = 1, N = 2, A = 3
3. D = 3, N = 2, A = 1
4. D = 1, N = 2, A = 3
5. D = 3, N = 2, A = 1
6. D = 3, N = 2, A = 1
7. D = 1, N = 2, A = 3
8. D = 1, N = 2, A = 3
9. D = 3, N = 2, A = 1
10. D = 3, N = 2, A = 1

Interpretation

25–30 Very positive attitudes toward helping, developing, and training others in the workplace. Such attitudes reflect strong teamwork and a compassion for the growth needs of others.

16–24 Mixed positive and negative attitudes toward helping, developing, and training others in the workplace. You may need to develop more sensitivity to the growth needs of others to be considered a strong team player.

10–15 Negative attitudes toward helping, developing, and training others in the workplace. Guard against being so self-centered that it will be held against you.

chances of finding your car will increase substantially. In short, tell your group member or protégé to intend to remember.

4. Encourage Learners to Practice and Rehearse the New Material

Those of you who have studied a foreign language or used new software are well aware of how important practice is for learning. Very little learning takes place unless you practice the new skill and rehearse the new knowledge. If you want to retain the information for just a minute or two, the most effective device is rote rehearsal. You recite the information to yourself silently or out loud several times.

For longer-term retention, it is usually necessary to use elaborative rehearsal—relating something to information we already know. Suppose a learner encounters the term *Intranet* in relation to information systems. He decides to store the word in long-term memory because it seems important. (*Intranet* refers to an information system within an organization, as opposed to the worldwide *Internet*.) The learner therefore makes the association of an internal network because *intra* reminds him of *intravenous* feeding, which involves putting a needle inside the vein.

5. Use Distributed Practice

An effective way of learning something is a little bit at a time. Most people retain more, and thus make better use of training, when they break up learning with frequent rest periods. Suppose you were training a coworker in the full details of preparing customer invoices. It would probably be better to work on these complicated procedures 30 minutes at a time than to spend five-hour blocks on training.

6. Ensure the Meaningfulness of Material

The material to be learned should be organized in a **meaningful** manner. Each successive experience should build on the other. In training another person how to process a customer order, you might teach the skill in terms of the flow of activities from customer inquiry to product delivery.

7. Give Feedback on Progress

As a person's training progresses, maintain and enhance motivation by providing knowledge on progress. To measure progress, it may be necessary to ask the trainee questions or ask for a job sample. For example, you might ask the person being trained on invoices to prepare a sample invoice.

8. Deal with Trainee Defensiveness

Training is sometimes retarded because the person being trained is defensive about information or skills that clash with his or her beliefs and practices. The person might have so much emotional energy invested in the status quo that he or she resists the training. For example, a sales representative might resist learning how to use e-commerce because she believes that her warm smile and interpersonal skills have made her an excellent communicator. She is concerned that if she communicates with customers exclusively through email, her human touch will be lost. Sensing this defensiveness, the trainer is advised to talk about e-commerce as being a supplement to, but not a substitute for, in-person communication. (However, the sales rep might also be worried that her position will be eliminated.)

9. Rely on the Magic Number Seven

The immediate **memory span** of an adult seems fixed at about seven items. Most people can remember up to about seven categories of most things. It is probably not coincidental that we have seven days of the week, seven primary colors, seven deadly sins, and seven notes on the musical scale. When you are trying to teach people new information, arrange it into seven large chunks. New bits of information can be added to one of these seven chunks.

10. Encourage Learners to Reflect on What They Have Learned

Current research indicates that if people think carefully about what they have learned, their retention of information increases. The idea is to step back from the experience to ponder carefully and persistently the meaning to a person.[1] After participating in a team development exercise involving white-water rafting, a person might reflect, "What did I really learn about being a better team player?" How was I perceived by teammates in the rubber raft? Did they even notice my contribution? Or did they think I was an important part of the team success?"

11. Encourage Informal Learning

As a coach or mentor, you should encourage your target people to learn in a variety of ways. In addition to training programs and direct coaching, substantial learning takes place outside of the classroom or away from the computer. Many employees learn job skills and information by asking each other questions, sharing ideas, and observing each other. Such learning is spontaneous, immediate, and task specific. Much **informal learning** takes place in meetings, on breaks, and in customer interactions.

A nationwide survey found that up to 70 percent of employee learning takes place informally.[2] At Siemens, a high-technology company, managers found that software developers acquired considerable job information by congregating in the company cafeteria. Some companies have now installed high round tables around the company so workers can informally exchange ideas in addition to small talk.

12. Recognize Differences in Learning Style

Another key factor that influences training is **learning style,** the way in which a person best learns new information. An example of a learning style is passive learning. People who learn best through passive learning quickly acquire information by studying texts, manuals, and magazine articles. They can juggle images in their mind as they read about abstract concepts such as supply and demand, cultural diversity, or customer service. Others learn best by doing rather than by studying—for example, learning about customer service by dealing with customers in many situations.

Another key dimension of learning styles is whether a person learns best by working alone or cooperatively, as in a study group. Learning by oneself may allow for more intense concentration, and one can proceed at one's own pace. Learning in groups and through classroom discussion allows people to exchange viewpoints and perspectives. Considerable evidence has been accumulated that peer tutoring and cooperative learning are effective for acquiring knowledge. Another advantage of cooperative learning is that it is more likely to lead to changes in behavior. Assume that a manager holds group discussions about the importance of achieving high customer satisfaction. Employees participating in these group discussions are more likely to assertively pursue high customer satisfaction on the job than those who only read about the topic.

Because of differences in learning styles, you may decide to design training to fit those differences. For example, if your trainees prefer cooperative learning you could combine learning from reading books, articles, and online material with discussions in the training room.

Think It Through   **What We Need Around Here is Better Human Relations**

Hank called his three highest-ranking managers together for a surprise luncheon meeting. "Have a healthy lunch on International Auto Parts," said Hank. "You may need it to loosen up your thinking about an important topic I want to bring to your attention."

After Madeline, Ray, and Allan ordered their lunch, Hank launched into the agenda.

Continued

As vice president of administration, I think we have to move into a rigorous human relations training program for our front-line supervisors and team leaders. It's no longer a question of whether we should have a program, it's now a question of what kind and when."

Allan spoke out, "Okay, Hank, don't keep us in suspense any longer. What makes you think we need a human relations training program?"

Look at the problems we are facing. Thirty-five percent turnover among the clerical support staffs and productivity lower than the automotive manufacturing industry standards. What better reasons could anybody have for properly training our supervisors and team leaders?

Madeline commented, "Hold on Hank. Training may not be the answer. I think our high turnover and low productivity are caused by reasons beyond the control of supervision. Our wages are low, and we expect our people to work in cramped, rather dismal office space."

Hank retorted, "Nonsense. A good supervisor can get workers to accept almost any working conditions. Training will fix that."

"Hank, I see another problem," said Allan. "Our supervisors and team leaders are so overworked that they will balk at training. If you hold the training on company time, they will say that they are falling behind in their work. If the training takes place after hours or on weekends, our supervisors and team leaders will say that they are being exploited."

"Not true," replied Hank. "Every supervisor or team leader realizes the importance of good human relations. Besides that, they will see the training as a form of job enrichment."

"So long as we are having an open meeting, let me give my input," volunteered Ray. "We are starting from the wrong end by having our first-line supervisors and team leaders go through human relations training. It's our top management who needs the training the most. Unless they practice better human relations, you can't expect such behavior from our supervisors. How can you have a top management group that is insensitive to people and a first-level management that is sensitive? The system just won't work."

"What you say makes some sense," said Hank, "but I wouldn't go so far as to say top management is insensitive to people. Maybe we can talk some about the human relations training after lunch."

Questions

1. Should Hank go ahead with his plans for the human relations training program? Why or why not?

2. What do you think of the merits of Ray's comment that top management should participate in human relations training first?

3. If you were in Hank's situation, would you try to get top management to participate in human relations training?

4. Which learning principles might be the most applicable to the proposed human relations training program?

Summary

Training is the process of helping others acquire a job-related skill. Everyone who serves as a coach and a mentor needs to know how to train others. There are eleven time-tested principles of learning that should always be considered when training: (1) encouraging concentration, (2) using motivated interest, (3) encouraging the intention to remember, (4) encouraging practice and rehearsal, (5) using distributed practice, (6) ensuring the meaningfulness of material, (7) giving feedback on progress, (8) dealing with trainee defensiveness, (9) relying on the magic number seven, (10) encouraging reflection on what is learned, (11) encouraging informal learning, and (12) recognizing differences in learning style.

Key Terms and Concepts

Informal learning   Meaningful

Learning   Memory span

Learning style   Training

Expand Your View

Skill-Building Exercise: Designing a Training Program

The class organizes into training-design teams of approximately six people. Each team sketches the design of a training program to teach an interpersonal skill to employees, such as being polite to customers or interviewing job candidates. The teams are not responsible for selecting the exact content of the training program they choose. Instead, they are responsible for designing a training program based on the principles of learning. The activity should take about 15 minutes and can therefore be done inside or outside of class. After the teams have designed their programs, they can compare the various versions.

Questions

1. Explain your position on whether workers have a responsibility to help each other grow and develop.
2. Why is there more emphasis today than in the past on workers helping each other grow and develop?
3. Do you think trainee defensiveness is a bigger problem in teaching technical or interpersonal skills? Explain.

Keeping Your Memory Sharp

Almost everyone experiences some memory loss with aging, and this slight impairment in memory can begin as early as the 30s. Typically the decrease in memory efficiency begins in the mid-40s or early 50s. A major contributor to memory loss is a decrease in the efficiency of brain cells. In normal aging, people suffer from a "tip-of-the-tongue" loss, such as not being able to remember the name of a movie they saw four months ago. Such a decrease in efficiency is not the same as Alzheimer's disease, in which people lose names of common objects such as "brick" or "ball-point pen," or of family members.

Another major contributor to memory loss once human beings reach age 50 is the shrinking of the hippocampus, the portion of the brain responsible for creating, storing, and accessing new information. As a result the brain's ability to process information slows, leading to common mistakes such as missing keys, wallets, and handbags.[3]

Short-term memory is likely to be much more affected by aging than is long-term memory. This explains why some people in their 70s might be able to provide details of their childhood but cannot recall a news story they watched on television three hours ago. A major contributor to short-term memory loss is that so much brain power is consumed in multitasking (coping with many responsibilities at once). Many people in their 40s, for example, hold a full-time job, have family responsibilities, are attending school part-time, and are constantly adapting to new technology.[4]

The reasons surrounding memory loss are complex, and some memory loss with aging is almost inevitable. Therefore, it is not realistic to think that a handful of techniques can entirely reverse memory loss. Nevertheless, certain steps to combat memory loss are backed by extensive research. Consider the following concepts and techniques to preserve your memory:[5]

1. *Use it or lose it.* People who continue to stretch their minds with new learning suffer much less memory loss than people who minimize intellectual challenge. Many famous scientists, professors, financiers, politicians, movie producers, and athletic coaches are people in their 70s.

2. *Be well organized.* People who carefully organize their work areas and personal items can compensate for short-term memory loss. For example, if you have one place for parking your keys, wallet, or

Continued

120

handbag, you are less likely to misplace such items. Concentrating on one activity at a time not only facilitates learning, it also helps ward off memory loss.

- *Exercise regularly.* Physical exercise builds both the body and the mind simultaneously. An extensive study showed that women who walk regularly are less likely to experience the memory loss and other declines in mental functioning associated with age. Researchers tracked 5,925 women age 65 and older and then studied them again six to eight years later. About 25 percent of the women who walked the least had a significant decline in mental ability test scores, compared with only 17 percent of the most active groups. Burning calories in other ways, such as tennis or golf, also had a positive effect on cognitive abilities.

- *Practice memory improvement techniques.* Memorization techniques such as making visual associations between new ideas and familiar objects and immediately rehearsing new material help combat memory loss. Writing down important dates and creating to-do lists can also help. The techniques found in books and courses about memory improvement work well if you remember to use them!

- *Take food supplements associated with memory preservation.* Many food supplements are available that are backed by claims of preserving the brain and improving memory. Antioxidants, particularly vitamin E, are a leading protective agent against neuron damage. (An antioxidant combats the harmful effects of oxidation on human tissue.) Impressive claims have also been made for ginkgo biloba, a brain pill for aging memories, concentration, absentmindedness, confusion, dizziness, and Alzheimer's disease.

In addition to the techniques and food supplements just listed, drugs and hormones have been developed that show promise of slowing down mental deterioration associated with age. An example is that a number of anti-inflammatory drugs, including arthritis drugs, are being tested to see if they reduce brain inflammation, another cause of neuron damage and death. No matter how successful these drugs, it will still be important to combat memory loss through the application of techniques of learning.

How does the above information relate to training? The link is that people with sharp memories train better!

4. Why is it often easier to train people in technical than in interpersonal skills?

5. Suppose you are coaching a 64-year-old man in your office, and he says, "I'm too old to learn." How would you deal with this attitude?

6. How might informal learning be used to supplement formal learning on the job?

7. What kind of experiment might a trainer conduct in the workplace that would verify whether or not a food supplement like ginkgo biloba actual improves the short-term memory of working adults?

Notes

1. Kent W. Siebert, "Reflection in Action: Tools for Cultivating On-the-Job Learning Conditions," *Organizational Dynamics* (Winter 1999), 55.

2. Nancy Day, "Informal Learning Gets Results," *Workforce* (June 1998), 31.

3. Catherine Arnst, "How to Keep Your Memory Intact," *Business Week* (October 15, 2001), 128E4.

4. Monika Guttman, "Are You Losing Your Mind?", *USA Weekend*, (May 16–18), 4–6; Dharma Singh Khalsa and Cameron Stauth, *Brain Longevity* (New York: Warner Books, 1998).

5. Guttman, "Are You Losing Your Mind?", 5; Arnst, "How to Keep Your Memory Sharp", 128E4–128E6; "Walking Can Keep Female Minds Sharp," *Gannett News Service*, (May 20, 2001).

Learning Links

Caudron, Shari. "Training and the ROI of Fun." *Workforce*, December 2000, 34–39.

Coutu, Diane L. "Too Old to Learn?" *Harvard Business Review*, November–December 2000, 37–52.

Edmondson, Amy, Richard Bohmer, and Gary Pisano. "Speeding Up Team Learning." *Harvard Business Review*, October 2001, 125–132.

Feeney, Shelea Anne. "Developing a New Generation of Public-agency Leaders. *Workforce*, November 2003, 79–80.

Frase-Blunt, Martha. "Ready, Set, Rotate!" *HR Magazine*, October 2001, 46–53.

Garvey, Charlotte. "The Whirlwind of a New Job." *HR Magazine*, June 2001, 110–118.

Patel, Dave. "Do More Than Train." *HR Magazine*, September 2001, 208.

Tyler, Kathryn. "Inadequate 'Air Rage' Training at Most Airlines Puts Employees at Risk." *HR Magazine*, September 2001, 64–74.

Zimmerman, Eilene. "Better Training Is Just a Click Away." *Workforce*, January 2001, 36–42.

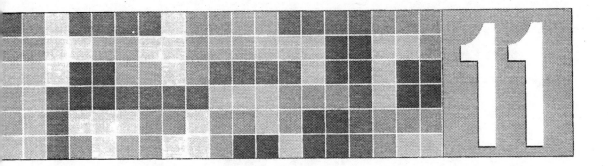

Helping Others Solve Problems

PERFORMANCE GOALS

After studying this chapter and doing the exercises, you should be able to:

- consider the personal characteristics of the problem solver.

- help others use a systematic approach to problem solving.

- establish the conditions necessary for creativity.

- prompt others to use creative problem-solving techniques.

- ask good questions to improve problem solving.

*"Sorry honey, I can't leave the office until I reach
my idea quota for the day."*

UNDERSTANDING PROBLEM SOLVING

In today's complex and rapidly changing business environment, the collective intelligence of group members is needed to solve problems. Solutions generated from the people actually doing the work can streamline processes and improve productivity. Many organizations encourage that teams solve key work problems. Therefore an important skill of a successful coach is to facilitate problem solving.

Developing the ability to solve problems well also helps employees advance their careers as they are able to contribute more to the team and their company. A good mentor will encourage his or her protégé to develop this ability to the fullest capability.

HELPING OTHERS SOLVE PROBLEMS

Problem solving can be a complex process; hence, teaching someone how to do it also involves many elements. There are several strategies and techniques to consider as you guide the people you coach or mentor toward effective problem solving.

1. Consider the Personal Characteristics of the Problem Solver

Personal characteristics can influence a team member's ability to solve problems. A good coach must take these characteristics into account for each individual. You may need to work with your team member or person you are mentoring to strengthen or weaken some of these characteristics to develop his or her problem-solving ability. (See Exhibit 11.1)

ARE YOU READY?   My Problem-Solving Tendencies

Directions: Describe how well you agree with the following statements. Use the following scale: disagree strongly (DS); disagree (D); neutral (N); agree (A); agree strongly (AS).

	DS	D	N	A	AS
1. Before reaching a final decision on a matter of significance, I like to discuss it with one or more other people.	1	2	3	4	5
2. If I'm facing a major decision, I like to get away from others to think it through.	5	4	3	2	1
3. I get lonely working by myself.	1	2	3	4	5
4. Two heads are better than one.	1	2	3	4	5
5. A wide range of people should be consulted before an executive makes a major decision.	1	2	3	4	5
6. To arrive at a creative solution to a problem, it is best to rely on a group.	1	2	3	4	5
7. From what I've seen so far, group decision making is a waste of time.	5	4	3	2	1
8. Most great ideas stem from the solitary effort of great thinkers.	5	4	3	2	1
9. Important legal cases should be decided by a jury rather than by a judge.	1	2	3	4	5
10. Individuals are better suited than groups to solve technical problems.	5	4	3	2	1

Total Score _____

Continued

Scoring and Interpretation: Add the numbers you circled to obtain your total score.

46–50:   You have strong positive attitudes toward group problem solving and decision making. You will therefore adapt well to the decision-making techniques widely used in organizations. Be careful, however, not to neglect your individual problem-solving skills.

30–45:   You have neutral attitudes toward group problem solving and decision making. You may need to remind yourself that group problem solving is well accepted in business.

10–29:   You much prefer individual to group decision making. Retain your pride in your ability to think independently, but do not overlook the contribution of group problem solving and decision making. You may need to develop more patience for group problem solving and decision making.

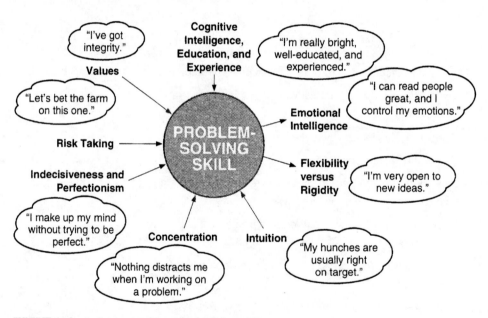

EXHIBIT 11.1   Influences on problem-solving skill.

■ *Cognitive intelligence, education, and experience.* The more **cognitive intelligence,** education, and experience your team member or protégé possesses, the better decisions he or she will make. Cognitive intelligence helps because, by definition, intelligence denotes the ability to solve problems. Education improves the problem-solving and decision-making process because it gives the problem solver a background of principles and facts to rely on. **Experience** facilitates decision making because good decisions tend to be made by people who have already faced similar situations in the past.

■ *Emotional intelligence.* This characteristic is important for decision making because effectiveness in managing feelings and reading other people can affect the quality of decisions. **Emotional intelligence** refers to qualities such as understanding one's own feelings, empathy for others, and the regulation of emotion to enhance living. This type of intelligence has to do with the ability to connect with people and understand their emotions. Being able to deal effectively with your own feelings and emotions and those of others can help you make better decisions.

■ *Flexibility.* Some people are successful problem solvers and decision makers because they approach every problem with a fresh outlook. This **flexibility** allows them to think of original—and therefore creative—alternative solutions to a problem. Another perspective on the same issue is that being open-minded helps a person solve problems well.

■ *Intuition.* Effective decision makers do not rely on careful analysis alone. Instead, they also use their **intuition,** a method of arriving at a conclusion by a quick judgment or gut feeling. Relying on intuition is like relying on instinct when faced with a decision. Intuition takes place when the brain gathers information stored in memory and packages it as a new insight or solution. Intuitions, therefore, can be regarded as stored information that is reorganized or repackaged. Developing good intuition may take a long time because so much information has to be stored.

■ *Concentration.* Being able to concentrate helps problem solvers pay attention to the details that may be necessary for a good decision. Mental **concentration** is an important contributor to making good decisions. Many people who solve problems poorly do so because they are too distracted to immerse themselves in the problem at hand. If the problem solver fails to concentrate hard enough, he or she may overlook an important detail that could affect the outcome of the decision.

■ *Indecisiveness and perfectionism.* **Indecision** and perfectionism can distract from and slow down problem solving. Some people are ill suited to solving problems and making decisions because they are fearful of committing themselves to any given course of action. People can be indecisive because they are perfectionists. In regard to decision making, **perfectionism** is a pattern of behavior in which the individual strives to accomplish unattainable standards of flawless work. Perfectionism leads people toward indecisiveness and delay in making decisions because they usually believe that they need more information before making a choice. The combination of being an indecisive person and a perfectionist can lead to **procrastination.** Also, being a procrastinator can make one indecisive.

■ *Risk taking.* The amount of **risk taking** your team member is willing to accept can lead to quick action that can be either positive or negative. For some types of problems, the risk taker or thrill seeker is at an advantage. For example, firefighters have to take risks to save people from burning buildings and to remove people trapped in collapsed buildings. Another example would be an information technology specialist who might have to engage in a risky maneuver to salvage data from a crashed hard drive. Risk taking can also lead to poor problem solving and decision making, such as a merchandiser buying a huge inventory of a highly original fashion. The experienced problem solver needs to know when to take high risks and when to be more conservative.

■ *Values.* **Values** influence decision making at every step. The values of the problem solver contribute to the positive or negative outcomes of a decision. The right values for the situation will improve problem solving and decision making, whereas the wrong values will lead to poor decisions. An example of a right value is the pursuit of excellence. A worker who embraces the pursuit of excellence (and is therefore conscientious) will search for the high-quality alternative solution. An example of a wrong value is attempting to preserve the status quo. A worker who clings to the status quo may fail to make a decision that could bring about major improvements.[1] Ultimately, all decisions are based on values.

2. Use a Systematic Approach to Problem Solving

The probability of solving the problem well (and therefore making the right decision) increases when a systematic procedure is used. The following guidelines represent a time-tested way of solving problems and making decisions, especially for teams.[2] These steps are best applied to complex problems. Straightforward problems of minor consequence (such as deciding on holiday decorations for the office) do not require all the steps.

■ *Step 1: Identify the problem.* Have your problem solver(s) describe specifically what the problem is and how it manifests itself. The surface problem is that some customers are paying their bills late. Your company's ultimate problem is that it does not have enough cash on hand to pay expenses.

■ *Step 2: Clarify the problem.* In a group setting, if team members do not see the problem the same way, they will offer divergent solutions to their own individual perceptions of the problem. To some team members, late payments may simply mean the company has less cash in the bank. As a result, the company earns a few dollars less in interest. Someone else on the team might perceive the problem as mostly an annoyance and inconvenience. Another person may perceive late payers as being immoral and therefore want to penalize them. It is important for the group to reach consensus that the ultimate problem is not enough cash on hand to run the business, as explained in Step 1.

■ *Step 3: Analyze the cause.* To convert what exists into what is desired, the problem solver(s) must understand the cause of the specific problems and find ways to overcome the causes. Late payment of bills (over 30 days) can be caused by several factors. The customers may have cash flow problems of their own, they may have slow-moving bureaucratic procedures, or they may be understaffed. Another possibility is that the slow-paying customers are dissatisfied with the service and are holding back on payments in retaliation. Research, including interviewing customers, may be needed to analyze the cause or causes.

■ *Step 4: Search for alternative solutions.* Remember that multiple alternative solutions can be found to most problems. The alternative solutions the problem solver(s) chooses will depend on the analysis of the causes. Assume it was found that customers were not dissatisfied with the company's service but that they were slow in paying bills for a variety of reasons. The problem solver(s) then gets into a creative mode by developing a number of alternatives. Among them are offering bigger discounts for quick payment, dropping slow-paying customers, sending out your own bills more promptly, and using follow-up phone calls to bring in money. Another possibility would be to set up a line of credit that would enable your firm to make short-term loans to cover expenses until your bills were paid.

■ *Step 5: Select alternatives.* Help your problem solver(s) identify the criteria that solutions should meet and then discuss the pros and cons of the proposed alternatives. No solution should be laughed at or scorned. Specifying the criteria that proposed solutions should meet requires thinking deeply about the intended goals. For example, your team might establish the criteria that proposed solutions should (1) improve cash flow, (2) not lose customers, (3) not cost much to implement, and (4) not make the company appear desperate. The pros and cons of each proposed alternative can be placed on a flip chart, chalkboard, or computer screen.

■ *Step 6: Plan for implementation.* Help the problem solver(s) decide what actions are necessary to carry out the chosen solution to the problem. Suppose your team decides that establishing a bank line of credit is the most feasible alternative. The company president or the chief financial officer might then meet with a couple of local banks to apply for a line of credit at the most favorable rate. Your group also chooses to initiate a program of friendly follow-up telephone calls to encourage more rapid payment.

■ *Step 7: Clarify the contract.* In a team setting, the contract is a restatement of what group members have agreed to do and deadlines for accomplishment. In an individual coaching situation, the contract can be set between you and that individual. In the situation discussed above, several team members are involved in establishing a line of credit and in initiating a system of follow-up phone calls.

■ *Step 8: Develop an action plan.* Specify who does what and when to carry out the contract. Each person involved in implementing alternatives develops an **action plan** in detail that stems logically from the previous step.

■ *Step 9: Provide for evaluation and accountability.* After the plan is implemented, reconvene with your problem solver(s) to discuss progress and to hold

ACTIVATE YOUR SKILLS: A General Problem-Solving Group

The class is divided into groups of about six people. Each group takes the same complicated problem through the nine steps for effective group decision making. Several of the steps will be hypothetical because this is a simulated experience. Pretend you are a task force composed of people from different departments in the company. Choose one of the following possibilities:

- *Scenario 1:* Your company wants your task force to decide whether to purchase a corporate jet for members of senior management or require them to continue to fly on commercial airlines.

- *Scenario 2:* You are employed by Eastman Kodak Company, the film and digital imaging giant. Data supplied by the marketing research department indicate that the consumption of film by consumers worldwide is declining. At the same time, digital photography is increasing. Your task force is asked to recommend a plan for increasing the consumption of film.

people accountable for results that have not been achieved. In the situation at hand, progress will be measured in at least two objective ways. You can evaluate by accounting measures whether the cash flow problem has improved and whether the average cycle time on accounts receivable has decreased.

3. Establish the Conditions Necessary for Creativity

In many work situations, employees are expected to produce creative and imaginative solutions to problems. Simply put, **creativity** is the ability to develop good ideas that can be put into action. Finding a creative idea usually involves a flash of insight about how to solve a problem. When people see or hear the word *creativity* many think of a rarefied talent. A more helpful perspective is to recognize that not all creativity requires wild imagination.

Creativity is not just a random occurrence. Well-known creativity researcher Teresa M. Amabile has summarized 22 years of her research about creativity in the workplace. Her findings are supported by others.[3] Creativity takes place when three internal components come together: expertise, creative-thinking skills, and the right type of motivation. **Expertise** refers to the necessary knowledge to put facts together. The more ideas floating around in the problem solver's head, the more likely he or she is to combine them in some useful way. **Creative thinking** refers to how flexibly

Creativity and marketing speaker Floyd Hunt has developed a test to see whether you have been lulled into complacency and therefore are not thinking creatively.

For each statement, rank yourself on the following 10-point scale:

I can't remember	1–2 points
Not in the past year	3–4 points
Sometime in the past year	5–6 points
In the past month	7–8 points
It happens often	9–10 points

The last time I remember . . .

1. Someone saying to me, "You've never done that before!" _____

2. Changing my routine for no particular reason other than I just wanted to _____

3. Rearranging my office, living room, or sock drawer just for fun _____

4. Someone telling me, "It can't be done," and my trying anyway _____

5. Fighting for an idea _____

6. Feeling that I was way out on a limb _____

7. Being told, "You're wrong," because I tried something new _____

8. Being wrong _____

9. Doing something that made me nervous _____

10. Feeling afraid and exhilarated at the same time _____

Scoring

Less than 20:	Get your head out of the sand.
21–50:	You have potential, but your routines need to be shaken up.
51–80:	You've either reached or are heading for success; watch out for becoming too complacent.
81–100:	Let me get out of your way!

Source: "Success Quiz," *Success*, November 1998, p. 22.

and imaginatively individuals approach problems. If the problem solver knows how to keep digging for alternatives and how to avoid getting stuck in the status quo, the chances of being creative multiply. Along these same lines, the problem solver is much more likely to be creative if he or she intentionally seeks ideas, such as always being on the lookout for money-saving ideas.

Persevering, or sticking with a problem to a conclusion, is essential for finding creative solutions. A few rest breaks to gain a fresh perspective may be helpful, but the creative person keeps coming back until a solution emerges. The right type of **motivation** is the third essential ingredient for creative thought. A fascination with or passion for the task is much more important than searching for external rewards. People will be most creative when they are motivated primarily by the satisfaction and challenge of the work itself. Passion for the task and high intrinsic motivation contribute to a total absorption in the work and intense concentration.

Although the coach may only somewhat influence the internal conditions fostering creativity, he or she can establish four external conditions that are key to creativity: necessity, conflict and tension, encouragement, and humor.

Creative condition 1.   An environmental need must stimulate the setting of a goal. This is another way of saying that necessity is the mother of invention. For example, several years ago, independent hardware stores were faced with the challenge of large chains, such as Home Depot and Lowe's, driving them out of business. Many of these independent stores survived by forming buying alliances with each other so they could purchase inventory in larger quantities—and therefore at lower prices. You can either communicate, or have your team members identify, the necessity.

Creative condition 2.   Another condition that fosters creativity is enough **conflict and tension** to put people on edge. Jerry Hirschberg, founder and president of Nissan Design International, says that a person should be asked to hold apparently conflicting ideas simultaneously. The opposition should be encouraged to do the same. Understanding opposing ideas helps people gain a new perspective. Some automobile designers were arguing about how to satisfy the conflicting consumer demands of having more storage space in an SUV without adding length. The demands seemed incompatible until one engineer flashed on an answer—a simple vertical rack of shelves that would provide ample storage space without increasing the length.[4] You should encourage each problem solver to develop conflicting ideas at the same time and support the expression of conflicting ideas in your group.

Creative condition 3.   Another external factor for creativity is **encouragement,** including a permissive atmosphere that welcomes new ideas. A coach who encourages imagination and original thinking and does not punish people for making honest mistakes is likely to receive creative ideas from people. For example, 3M is highly regarded as a company with many innovations in addition to Scotch tape and Post-it notes. The company encourages creativity in many ways, such as granting people time off from regular responsibilities just to think about new ideas. Let your team members know you are open to hearing about imaginative ideas even if they may not work out and consider ways to encourage their creativity.

Creative condition 4.   Finally, **humor** is a key environmental condition for enhancing creativity. Humor has always been linked to creativity. Humor gets the creative juices flowing, and effective humor requires creativity. Thomas Edison started every workday with a joke-telling session. Mike Vance, chairman of the Creative Thinking Association of America, says that "Humor is unmasking the hypocritical. What makes us laugh often is seeing how things are screwed up—then sometimes seeing how we can fix them. Whenever I go into a company and don't hear much laughter, I know it's not a creative place."[5] Not only can you develop and use your sense of humor to foster creativity, you can encourage tactful and appropriate humor among team members.

4. Use Creative Problem-Solving Techniques

Encourage intense concentration.   The ability to concentrate was mentioned earlier as a characteristic that contributes to effective problem solving in general. The ability to eliminate distractions also contributes mightily to generating new ideas. At times we believe we are thinking intently about our problem, yet in reality we may be thinking about something that interferes

---

ARE YOU READY?   **Creative Personality Test**

Answer each of the following statements as "Mostly True" or "Mostly False." We are looking for general trends, so do not be concerned that under certain circumstances your answer might be different in response to a particular statement.

	Mostly true	Mostly false
1. I think novels are a waste of time, so I am more likely to read a nonfiction book.	_____	_____
2. You have to admit, some crooks are ingenious.	_____	_____
3. I pretty much wear the same style and colors of clothing regularly.	_____	_____
4. To me most issues have a clear-cut right side or wrong side.	_____	_____
5. I enjoy it when my boss hands me vague instructions.	_____	_____

Continued

6. When I'm surfing the Internet, I sometimes investigate topics I know very little about. _____ _____

7. Business before leisure activities is a hard and fast rule in my life. _____ _____

8. Taking a different route to work is fun, even if it takes longer. _____ _____

9. From time to time I have made friends with people of a different sex, race, religion, or ethnic background from myself. _____ _____

10. Rules and regulations should be respected, but deviating from them once in a while is acceptable. _____ _____

11. People who know me say that I have an excellent sense of humor. _____ _____

12. I have been known to play practical jokes or pranks on people. _____ _____

13. Writers should avoid using unusual words and word combinations. _____ _____

14. Detective work would have some appeal to me. _____ _____

15. I am much more likely to tell a rehearsed joke than make a witty comment. _____ _____

16. Almost all national advertising on television bores me. _____ _____

17. Why write letters to friends when there are so many clever greeting cards already available in the stores? _____ _____

18. For most important problems in life, there is one best solution available. _____ _____

19. Pleasing myself means more to me than pleasing others. _____ _____

20. I'm enjoying taking this test. _____ _____

Score: _____

Scoring: Give yourself a plus 1 for each answer scored in the creative direction as follows:

1. Mostly false	6. Mostly true	11. Mostly true	16. Mostly false
2. Mostly true	7. Mostly false	12. Mostly true	17. Mostly false
3. Mostly false	8. Mostly true	13. Mostly false	18. Mostly false
4. Mostly false	9. Mostly true	14. Mostly true	19. Mostly true
5. Mostly true	10. Mostly true	15. Mostly false	20. Mostly true

Interpretation: A score of 15 or more suggests that your personality and attitudes are similar to those of a creative person. A score of between 9 and 14 suggests an average similarity with the personality and attitudes of a creative person. A score of 8 or less suggests that your personality is dissimilar to that of a creative person. You are probably more of a conformist and not highly open-minded in your thinking at this point in your life. To become more creative, you may need to develop more flexibility in your thinking and a higher degree of open-mindedness.

with creativity.[6] Work with your team members to determine individual distractions and methods to avoid them.

Overcome traditional mental sets.   An important consequence of becoming more intellectually flexible is that one can overcome a **traditional mental set,** a fixed way of thinking about objects and activities. Overcoming traditional mental sets is important because the major block to creativity is to perceive things in a traditional way. An effective way of overcoming a traditional mental set (or **thinking outside the box**) is to challenge the status quo. Support the people you coach when they question the old standby that things have always been done in a particular way.

Encourage lateral thinking.   A major challenge in developing creative thinking skills is to learn how to think laterally in addition to vertically. **Vertical thinking** is an analytical, logical process that results in few answers. The vertical thinker is looking for the one best solution to a problem, much like solving an equation in algebra. In contrast, **lateral thinking** spreads out to find many alternative solutions to a problem. In short, critical thinking is vertical and creative thinking is lateral. To encourage lateral thinking, coach your team members to develop the mental set that every problem has multiple solutions. Have them sketch out many alternatives before walking away from the problem at hand.

Conduct brainstorming sessions.   The best-known method of improving creativity is **brainstorming,** a technique by which team members think of multiple solutions to a problem. Using brainstorming, a group of six people might sit around a table generating new ideas for a product. During the idea-generating part of brainstorming, potential solutions are not criticized or evaluated in any way. In this way spontaneity is encouraged. Rules for brainstorming are presented below. Brainstorming has many variations, including an electronic approach, creative twosomes, brainwriting, and forced associations.

Guidelines for Brainstorming

1. Group size should be about five to seven people. If there are too few people, not enough suggestions are generated; if there are too many people, the session becomes uncontrolled. However, brainstorming can be conducted with as few as three people.

2. Everybody is given the chance to suggest alternative solutions. Members spontaneously call out alternatives to the problem facing the group. (Another approach is for people to speak in sequence.)

3. No criticism is allowed. All suggestions should be welcome; it is particularly important not to use derisive laughter.

4. Freewheeling is encouraged. Outlandish ideas often prove quite useful. It's easier to tame a wild idea than to originate one.

5. Quantity and variety are very important. The greater the number of ideas put forth, the greater the likelihood of a breakthrough idea.

6. Combinations and improvements are encouraged. Building upon the ideas of others, including combining them, is very productive. "Hitchhiking" or "**piggybacking**" is an essential part of brainstorming.

7. Notes must be taken during the session by a person who serves as the recording secretary. The session can also be taped, but this requires substantial time to retrieve ideas.

8. Do not overstructure by following any of the seven ideas too rigidly. Brainstorming is a spontaneous group process.

An important strategy for enhancing the outcome of brainstorming is to have intellectually and culturally diverse group members. Some group leaders purposely choose people of different problem-solving styles (such as the reflective types and intuitive types) to encourage more diverse thinking. The reflective type might have more brainstorms based on facts, whereas the intuitive type may have more brainstorms based on hunches. Cultural **diversity** is likely to improve brainstorming because people with different cultural experiences often bring different viewpoints to bear on the problem. For example, when developing new food products, members with different ethnic backgrounds are chosen for a brainstorming group.

In **electronic brainstorming,** team members simultaneously enter their suggestions into a computer. The ideas are distributed to the screens of other team members. Although the team members do not talk to each other, they are still able to build on each other's ideas and combine ideas. Electronic brainstorming helps overcome certain problems encountered in traditional brainstorming. Shyness, domination by one or two members, and participants who loaf tend to be less troublesome than in face-to-face situations. Electronic brainstorming allows members to enter their ideas whenever they want, while sending along their ideas anonymously. These two features reduce the inhibitions caused by waiting for other people and by fear of negative evaluations.

Some of the advantages of brainstorming can be achieved by thinking through a challenging problem with a partner. **Creative twosomes** are a favorite of the music business (for example, Rodgers and Hammerstein). Many researchers work in twosomes. Part of the creative-twosome technique is to audiotape your problem-solving session. After exhausting your ideas, return and listen to your tape together. Listening to previous ideas helps spur new thoughts.

In many situations, brainstorming alone produces as many or more useful ideas as does brainstorming in groups. **Brainwriting,** or solo brainstorming, is arriving at creative ideas by jotting them down. The problem solver needs to develop mental flexibility for brainstorming. Self-discipline is very important for brainwriting because some people have a tendency to postpone something as challenging as thinking alone. An important requirement of brainwriting is that it must be done at a regular time (and perhaps place) for generating ideas. The ideas discovered in the process of routine activities can be counted as bonus time. Even five minutes a day is more time than most people are accustomed to spend thinking creatively about job problems.

A widely used method of releasing creativity is the **forced-association technique.** Using this technique, individuals or groups solve a problem by making associations between the properties of two objects. A link is found between the properties of the random object and the properties of the problem object. The forced association is supposed to help solve the problem. An individual (working alone or in a group) selects a word at random from a dictionary or textbook. If a preposition is chosen, have that person try again until a noun is found. Next, the person (or group) lists many of the properties and attributes of this word. Assume the randomly chosen word is *ladder*. Among its attributes are "durable," "foldable," "aluminum or wood," "moderately priced," and "easy to use." If the problem in front of the group is trying to improve a bow tie to increase sales, for example, solutions might include making the tie more durable and easier to use.

In the various types of brainstorming just discussed, collecting wild ideas is just the start of the process. After ideas are collected, the group or each member carefully evaluates and analyzes the various alternatives. It is usually important to also specify the implementation details. For example, how do you make a bow tie easier to use other than by adding a clip?

ACTIVATE YOUR SKILLS: 1–800–Insight

Using conventional brainstorming or one of its variations, huddle in small groups. Your task is to develop 800, 888, or 900 telephone numbers for firms in various fields. Keep in mind that the best 800 (or 888 or 900) numbers are easy to memorize and have a logical connection to the goods or services provided. After each group makes up its list of telephone numbers (perhaps about three for each firm on the list), compare results with the other groups. Here is the list of enterprises:

- A nationwide chain of funeral homes
- An air conditioning firm
- A software problem help line for Microsoft Corp.
- A used car chain
- A prayer service (a 900 number)
- An introduction (dating) service (a 900 number)

Advocate Borrowing Creative Ideas. Borrowing the successful ideas of others is a legitimate form of creativity. Be careful, however, that appropriate credit is given. Encourage your team members to keep careful records of these ideas and their sources so that they will not be forgotten. Knowing when and which ideas to borrow from other people can help your team members behave imaginatively. Creative ideas can be borrowed, for example, from the following sources:

- speaking to friends, relatives, classmates, and coworkers
- reading newspapers, newsmagazines, trade magazines, textbooks, nonfiction books, and novels
- surfing the Internet
- watching television and listening to radio programs
- subscribing to computerized information services (expensive, but worth it to many ambitious people)

Challenge Your Team Members' Ruts. A major hurdle to thinking creatively is getting locked into so many habits and routines that our thinking becomes too mechanical. According to Kathleen R. Allen, "We do the same things, the same way, every day. This is a primary barrier to creativity. Often we need to feel a little uncomfortable—we need to experience new things—to get creative sparks."[7] Challenging your team members' everyday **ruts,** or habitual way of doing things, can help them develop mental flexibility. Encourage them to think of ways or give them opportunities that force them out of their normal environment in order to see things in new and different ways. Avoiding ruts is closely associated with overcoming traditional mental sets. Traditional mental sets are essentially mental ruts. Here is a sampling of everyday ruts that could be challenged:

- Eating lunch with the same friends at work or school
- Watching the same television shows or reading only the same sections of the newspaper
- Restricting Internet browsing to the same few bookmarks
- Befriending only those people in one's own demographic group (e.g., age range, race, ethnic background)
- Engaging in the same pastimes exclusively
- Using the same form of physical exercise each time

Establish Idea Quotas. To enhance creativity, many companies assign **idea quotas** to workers. For example, workers might be instructed to bring one good idea for earning or saving money to every meeting. Establishing idea quotas is similar to brainwriting with a goal in mind. An easy way of getting started is to establish a monthly minimum quota of one creative idea to improve the job. Although this exercise might take only about five minutes of thinking each month, it could have a tremendous impact on productivity.

5. Ask Good Questions

Asking good questions is not only an effective active listening technique, it is also a good technique for encouraging problem solving. Asking open-ended questions rather than giving answers is the natural method of helping group members become better problem solvers. Here are sample questions a leader might ask group members to help them meet their challenges:

- What are you going to do differently to reduce by 50 percent the time it takes to fill a customer order?
- Top management is thinking of getting rid of our group and subcontracting the work we do to outside vendors. What do you propose we do to make us more valuable to the company?
- Can you figure out why the competition is outperforming us?

Think It Through   The Great Wiper Blade Mystery

It was a mystery—a mystery with millions of dollars and hundreds of jobs riding on the answer. A huge 6.5 percent of the windshield wiper systems being manufactured at an ITT automotive plant in upstate New York for DaimlerChrysler's minivans were defective. Nobody could figure out why the defect existed. All the parts met specifications; they were assembled correctly, and engineers found no fault with the design. Yet, in a test run, many wipers failed to make a complete sweep across the windshield—a potential disaster for Chrysler and for the 3,800 automotive workers in the upstate plant.

Plant management assembled a six-person team including engineers, union members, and manufacturing experts to become a detective force to find the answers. The team felt a lot of pressure to resolve the problem because the livelihood of the plant was threatened. If its major product was defective, the plant might be shuttered.

Technical Aspects of the Problem

The new wiper system was the biggest and most complex ever assembled in the plant. Instead of just delivering wiper blades, the local plant was given "black box responsibility" to deliver a perfectly functioning windshield system that Chrysler workers could just snap into place.

The blades, instead of moving right and left in tandem, came together in the center of the windshield and spread apart again, making timing a crucial issue. "The number of things that could go wrong were exponentially greater than for anything we had ever done before," said

Continued

Rob Price, manufacturing general supervisor. Just one thing did go wrong, but it was enough to threaten the project.

In 6.5 percent of the wipers, the blade's swing was up to 2.5 degrees short. That's equivalent to less than half a second on the face of a clock. But it was enough to make the blade fall short of sweeping the full area in front of the driver's face—an area that federal regulators insist be kept clear of rain and ice.

The Cross-Functional Team Tackles the Problem

Responsibility for solving the problem fell to the Chrysler cross-functional team: leader of the plant's Chrysler team Craig Hysong, manufacturing general supervisor Rob Price, quality technician Rick Fisher, quality analyst Jeannine Marciano, engineer Mike Kinsky, and Ron Maor, an engineer from a sister plant in Ontario, Canada. Each new ITT automotive product has its cross-functional team, drawn from the different departments. The team's goal was to make sure the product was launched flawlessly.

The Chrysler team picked the best and worst of the wipers—called "Bob" and "Wow" for the best of the best and the worst of the worst. They thought that by comparing the best with the worst, they might somehow isolate and fix the problem.

The team felt the pressure to perform because unless they solved the mystery, Chrysler would have to find a new supplier for windshield wiper systems. Finally, Fisher, the technician, and Maor, the engineer from the plant that supplies the motors, found the answer. It was in the serrations (rough marks, like those on a serrated knife) on the motor's drive shaft that are meant to hold the crank in place.

Questions

1. Which approach to (or method of) group problem solving did the plant team use?
2. To what extent did management make the right move in assigning the flawed windshield wiper problem to a team instead of to one engineer or technician?
3. If by chance you happen to have the right expertise, what would you guess was the problem with the windshield wiper system?

Case excerpted and paraphrased from Phil Ebersole, "ITT Automotive Sleuths Solve a Design Mystery," Rochester, New York, *Democrat and Chronicle*, May 4, 1997, pp. 1E, 4E.

Summary

Another critical skill for the coach and mentor is to facilitate and encourage group and independent problem solving. You can help develop your team members and protégés become better at problem solving by first considering the personal characteristics of the problem solver—cognitive intelligence, education, and experience; emotional intelligence; flexibility; intuition; concentration; indecisiveness and perfectionism; risk taking; and values.

To achieve the most success, you can then guide your team members through a systematic approach to problem solving: (1) identifying the problem, (2) clarifying the problem, (3) analyzing the cause, (4) searching for alternative solutions, (5) selecting alternatives, (6) planning for implementation, (7) clarifying the contract, (8) developing an action plan, and (9) providing for evaluation and responsibility.

You can also establish an environment that encourages creativity and problem solving by (1) showing a necessity for change, (2) allowing the expression of conflicting ideas, (3) encouraging imagination and original thinking, and (4) fostering tactful humor in the group.

Encouraging creative problem solving also facilitates effective problem solving. You can use such techniques as (1) encouraging intense concentration, (2) overcoming traditional mental sets, (3) thinking laterally, (4) conducting brainstorming sessions, including electronic brainstorming, creative twosomes, brainwriting, and forced associations, (5) borrowing creative ideas, including benchmarking, (6) challenging ruts, and (7) establishing idea quotas. Finally asking good questions instead of supplying answers to the people you coach or mentor is a simple technique to stimulate problem solving.

Key Terms and Concepts

Action plan

Asking good questions

Benchmarking

Borrowing

Brainstorming

Brainwriting

Cognitive intelligence

Concentration

Conflict and tension

Creative thinking

Creative twosomes

Creativity

Diversity

Electronic brainstorming

E-mail

Emotional intelligence

Encouragement

Evaluation apprehension

Experience

Expertise

Flexibility

Forced-association technique

Freewheeling

Humor

Idea quota

Imagination

Indecision

Intuition

Lateral thinking

Motivation

Perfectionism

Piggybacking

Procrastination

Risk taking

Ruts

Thinking outside the box

Traditional mental set

Values

Vertical thinking

Expand Your View

Self-Assessment Exercise: Rhyme and Reason

A noted creativity expert says that exercises in rhyming release creative energy; they stir imagination into action. While doing the following exercises, remember that rhyme is frequently a matter of sound and does not have to involve similar or identical spelling. This exercise deals with light and frivolous emotions. After each word or phrase, write two rhyming words to describe it.

Examples:

1. Obese feline	<u>Fat</u>	<u>cat</u>
2. Television	<u>Boob</u>	<u>tube</u>
3. A computer command tool for the home	<u>House</u>	<u>mouse</u>

Now try these:

1. Vehicle damage   _____   _____
2. Domestic insect   _____   _____
3. Software about gambling   _____   _____
4. Impolite young lady   _____   _____
5. Profit from sale of airplane   _____   _____
6. Beautiful pig   _____   _____
7. Garment for a simian   _____   _____
8. Wooden Australian man   _____   _____
9. Slumber at a discount motel   _____   _____
10. Inventory of timepieces   _____   _____
11. Cutting instrument for a bride   _____   _____
12. Jump by an awful person   _____   _____
13. Extensive experience   _____   _____
14. Criticism lacking in effectiveness   _____   _____
15. Last place team   _____   _____
16. Coloring for dessert   _____   _____
17. Courageous person who is owned as property by another   _____   _____
18. Jump off a building   _____   _____
19. Strange hair growing on the lower part of a man's face   _____   _____
20. Supporter of a computer criminal   _____   _____
21. A computer whiz with a ridiculous sense of humor   _____   _____

Answers and Interpretation: The more of these rhymes you were able to come up with, the higher your creative potential. You would also need an advanced vocabulary to score very high (for instance, what is a *simian?*). Ten or more correct rhymes would tend to show outstanding creative potential, at least in the verbal area. Here are the answers:

1. Fender bender	9. Cheap sleep	17. Brave slave
2. House louse	10. Clock stock	18. Tall fall
3. Risk disk	11. Wife knife	19. Weird beard
4. Crass lass	12. Creep leap	20. Hacker backer
5. Jet net	13. Vast past	21. Absurd nerd
6. Fine swine	14. Weak critique	
7. Ape cape	15. Cellar dweller	
8. Oak bloke	16. Pie die	

If you can think of a sensible substitute for any of these answers, give yourself a bonus point. For example, for number 21, how about a freak geek?

Source: The concept for this test traces back to Eugene Raudsepp with George P. Hough, Jr., *Creative Growth Games* (New York: Penguin, 1977). The current test contains just two of the original items.

Skill-Building Exercise: Brainstorming Versus Brainwriting

Half the class is organized into brainstorming groups of about six people. The rest of the class work by themselves. Groups and individuals then work on the same problems for 10 minutes. The brainstorming groups follow the aforementioned guidelines. Individuals jot down as many alternatives as come to mind without interacting with other people. After the problem-solving sessions are completed, compare the alternatives developed by the groups and the individuals.

Groups and individuals choose one of the following problems so that solutions can be compared to the same problems:

1. How might we effectively utilize the senior citizens in our community?
2. How can we earn extra money, aside from holding a regular job?
3. How can we find new people to date?
4. How can we save money on food costs?
5. How can we save money on gasoline?

Questions

1. What would be some of the symptoms or signs of a rigid thinker?
2. How might being a perfectionist create performance problems for a team leader? For a paralegal? For a computer programmer?
3. Why does concentration improve problem solving?

4. Why is intuition often referred to as a "sixth sense"?

5. Give an example of one work problem and one personal problem for which brainstorming might be useful.

6. Why are group decision-making skills so important for members of a work team?

7. Identify several problems on or off the job for which you think brainstorming would be effective.

Notes

1. John S. Hammond, Ralph L. Keeney, and Howard Rafia, "The Hidden Traps in Decision Making," *Harvard Business Review,* (September–October 1998), 50.

2. Andrew E. Schwartz and Joy Levin, "Better Group Decision Making," *Supervisory Management* (June 1990), 4.

3. Teresa M. Amabile, "How to Kill Creativity," *Harvard Business Review* (September–October 1998), 78–79.

4. Jerry Hirschberg, *The Creative Priority: Driving Innovative Business in the Real World* (New York: HarperBusiness, 1998).

5. Cited in Robert McGarvey, "Turn It On," *Entrepreneur* (November 1996), 156–157.

6. Frederick D. Buggie, "Overcoming Barriers to Creativity," *Innovative Leader* (May 1997), 5.

7. Quoted in Mark Hendricks, "Good Thinking: Knock Down the Barrier to Creativity—and Discover a Whole World of New Ideas," *Entrepreneur* (May 1996), 158.

Learning Links

Campbell, Donald J. "The Proactive Employee: Managing Workplace Initiative." *The Academy of Management Executive,* August 2000, 52–66.

"Creativity Training and Enhancement Information." www.selfgrowth.com/creativity.html (accessed December 6, 2003).

Garvin, David A., and Michael A. Roberto. "What You Don't Know About Making Decisions." *Harvard Business Review,* September 2001, 108–116.

Herbold, Robert J. "Inside Microsoft: Balancing Creativity and Discipline." *Harvard Business Review,* January 2002, 72–79.

"Problem Solving Through Coaching," www.extension.iastate.edu/efnep/problems.html (accessed December 6, 2002).

Sutton, Robert I. "The Weird Rules of Creativity." *Harvard Business Review,* September 2001, 94–103.

Zuckerman, Marvin. "Are You a Risk Taker?" *Psychology Today,* December 2000, 52–56, 84, 87.

Helping Difficult People

PERFORMANCE GOALS

After studying this chapter and doing the exercises, you should be able to:

- recognize that different types of difficult people exist.

- take problems professionally, not personally.

- listen and respond to the difficult person and criticize constructively.

- use tact, diplomacy, and humor to deal with the difficult person.

- work out a deal and reinforce civil behavior and good moods.

"I'd like to work out a deal with you. If you stop referring to me as a 'worthless number cruncher' in department meetings, I'll get you the new swivel chair you've always wanted."

UNDERSTANDING DIFFICULT PEOPLE

A challenge we all face from time to time is dealing constructively with team members who appear intent on creating problems. For a variety of reasons, these difficult or counterproductive people perform poorly themselves or interfere with the job performance of others. A **difficult person** is an individual who creates problems for others, yet has the skill and mental ability to do otherwise.

Types of Difficult People

Dozens of types of difficult people have been identified, with considerable overlap among the types. For example, one method of classifying difficult people might identify the *dictator*, while another method might identify the *bully*. Our purposes will be served by listing a sampling of the many types of difficult people found in the workplace and as customers.[1]

- **Know-it-alls** believe they are experts on everything. They have opinions on any issue; yet when they are wrong, they pass the buck or become defensive.

- **Blamers** are workers who never solve their own problems. When faced with a challenge or a hitch, they think the problem belongs to the supervisor or a group member.

- **Gossips** spread negative rumors about others and attempt to set people against each other.

- **Dictators** bully, cajole, and intimidate others. They are blunt to the point of being insulting. Dictators constantly make demands on workmates.

- **Repulsives** are people whose poor personal hygiene, eating habits, appearance, or foul language disrupt the tranquility of others.

- **Yes-people** agree to any commitment, promise any deadline, yet rarely deliver. Although sorry about being late, they cannot be trusted to deliver as promised.

- **No-people** are negative and pessimistic and quick to point out why something will not work. They are also inflexible, resist change, and complain frequently.

- **Jekyll and Hydes** have a split personality. When dealing with supervisors, customers, or clients, they are pleasant, engaging people; yet when carrying out the role of supervisors, they become tyrannical.

- **Backstabbers** pretend to befriend you and encourage you to talk freely about problems or personality clashes you face. Later, the backstabber reports the information—often in exaggerated form—to the person you mentioned in a negative light. Or the backstabber simply says negative things about you behind your back to discredit you to others.

- **Lone wolves** can't stand being part of anything: a team, a project, group functions. Independent to a fault, they make no attempt to hide solitary preferences.

- **Chicken Littles** always find a cloud to cast a shadow, no matter how sunny things seem to be. ("What a great website we have—20,000 visitors in the first week." "Yeah, but are more than one percent buying anything?")

EFFECTIVELY COACHING AND MENTORING DIFFICULT PEOPLE

It is possible to help difficult people grow, develop, and be more productive if you apply the following tactics. They do require practice to be effective. Also, you may have to use a combination of the six tactics described in this section to successfully coach a difficult person. The point of these tactics is not to outmanipulate or subdue a difficult person, but to establish a cordial and productive working relationship.

Directions: For each of the following scenarios, choose the method of handling the situation you think would be the most effective. Make a choice, even though more than one method of handling the situation seems plausible.

1. A coworker in the cubicle next to you is talking loudly on the telephone about the fabulous weekend she and a few friends enjoyed. You are attempting to deal with a challenging work problem. To deal with this situation, you

   a. Get up from your chair, stand close to her, and say loudly, "Shut up, you jerk. I'm trying to do my work."

   b. Slip her a handwritten note that says, "I'm happy that you had a great weekend, but I have problems concentrating on my work when you are talking so loudly. Thanks for your help."

   c. Get the boss on the phone and ask that she please do something about the problem.

   d. Wait until lunch and then say to her, "I'm happy that you had a great weekend, but I have problems concentrating on my work when you are talking so loudly. Thanks for your help."

2. One of your coworkers, Olaf, rarely carries his fair load of the work. He forever has a good reason for not having the time to do an assignment. This morning he has approached you to load some new software onto his personal computer. You deal with this situation by

   a. Carefully explaining that you will help him, providing he will take over a certain specified task for you.

   b. Telling him that you absolutely refuse to help a person as lazy as he is.

   c. Counseling him about fair play and reciprocity.

   d. Reviewing with him a list of five times at which he has asked other people to help him out. You then ask if he thinks this is a good way to treat coworkers.

3. In your role as supervisor, you have noticed that Diane, one of the group members, spends far too much work time laughing and joking. You schedule a meeting with her. As the meeting opens, you

   a. Joke and laugh with her to establish rapport.

   b. Explain to Diane that you have called this meeting to discuss her too-frequent laughing and joking.

   c. Talk for a few moments about the good things Diane has done for the department, then confront the real issue.

   d. Explain to Diane that she is on the verge of losing her job is she doesn't act more maturely.

Continued

4. As a team member, you have become increasingly annoyed with Jerry's ethnic, racist, and sexist jokes. One day during a team meeting, he tells a joke you believe is particularly offensive. To deal with the situation, you

    a. Meet privately with the team leader to discuss Jerry's offensive behavior.

    b. Catch up with Jerry later when he is alone, and tell him how uncomfortable his joke made you feel.

    c. Confront Jerry on the spot and say, "Hold on Jerry. I find your joke offensive."

    d. Tell the group an even more offensive joke to illustrate how Jerry's behavior can get out of hand.

5. You have been placed on a task force to look for ways to save the company money, including making recommendations for eliminating jobs. You interview a supervisor about the efficiency of her department. She suddenly becomes rude and defensive. In response, you

    a. Politely point our how her behavior is coming across to you.

    b. Get your revenge by recommending that three jobs be eliminated from her department.

    c. Explain that you have used up enough of her time for today and ask for another meeting later in the week.

    d. Tell her that unless she becomes more cooperative this interview cannot continue.

Scoring and Interpretation: Use the following key to obtain your score:

1.		2.		3		4		5	
a.	1	a.	4	a.	1	a.	2	a.	4
b.	4	b.	1	b.	4	b.	4	b.	1
c.	2	c.	3	c.	3	c.	3	c.	2
d.	3	d.	2	d.	2	d.	1	d.	3

18–20	You have good intuition about helping difficult people.
10–17	You have average intuition about helping difficult people.
5–9	You need to improve your sensitivity about helping difficult people.

1. Take Problems Professionally, Not Personally

A key principle in dealing with difficult people is to take what they do professionally, not personally. Difficult people are not necessarily out to get you. You may just represent a stepping-stone for them to get what they want.[2] For example, if a coworker insults you because you need his help on Friday afternoon, he probably has nothing against you personally; he may just prefer to become mentally disengaged from work that Friday afternoon. Your request distracts him from mentally phasing out of work as early as he would like.

2. Confront the Difficult Person

A good starting point for overcoming problems created by a difficult person is to confront that individual with his or her annoying or counterproductive behavior. In some instances, simply confronting the problem will make it go away. One supervisor said to a group member, "Please stop suggesting that we take two-hour lunch breaks every payday. It makes me tense to have to reject you." The requests for the luncheon sojourns stopped immediately.

A fundamental reason why we resist confronting another person, particularly a subordinate, about a sensitive issue is that we recognize how uncomfortable we feel when confronted by a boss. A manager who is about to confront a subordinate about irregularities on an expense account might say to himself, "I know how bad I would feel if I were told by my boss that I had been overcharging the company on trips. Maybe if I let it pass one more time, Jack [the subordinate] will shape up by himself."

Another reason many people are hesitant to confront another person is fear of a reprisal or quarrel. What specific kind of reprisal might occur is usually unknown, which makes the confrontation seem all the more hazardous. One member of a task force was going to confront another with the opinion that the latter was not carrying her fair share, thus increasing the burden for other members of the task force. The would-be confronter backed off, thinking that the woman confronted might tell lies about her to their mutual boss.

Seven suggestions may ease the confrontation process.[3] Since confrontation of some sort is a vital step in attempting to influence the behavior of another individual, they are worth giving serious thought.

a. *Being with a clear perception of what constitutes acceptable behavior.* Confrontation makes more sense when you have specific ideas of the limits to acceptable behavior. The widespread problem of incivility is a case in point. Given that many people are rude, you may need flexible standards of what constitutes serious incivility. You might decide, for example, that a person who consistently blocks the doorway while rambling about personal matters is being uncivil. Or you might have a clear idea of what type of swearing is acceptable in the office. Company policy can often be consulted to help define what constitutes unacceptable behavior.

b. *Attempt to relax during the confrontation session.* If you appear overly tense, you might communicate through body language that you lack confidence. Sometimes a rehearsal interview with a friend will be helpful in reducing your tension.

c. *Get to the central purpose of your meeting almost immediately.* Too often when people attempt to confront somebody about a sensitive issue, they waste time talking about unrelated topics. Discussions about vacations, professional sports, or business conditions have some value as warm-up material for other kinds of interviews but are inappropriate here.

d. *Avoid being apologetic or defensive.* You have a right to demand constructive relationships with other people in your work environment. For instance, there is no need to say, "Perhaps I may be way off base, but it seems like you slam the door shut every time I can't process your request immediately." Let the door-slamming coworker correct you if your observations are inaccurate.

e. *Confront the other individual in a nonhostile manner.* Confrontations about counterproductive behavior should be conducted with feeling (particularly sincerity), but not with hostility. Confrontations are associated with bitter conflict so frequently that the very word connotes hostility. Yet all forms of confrontation need not be conflagrations. Hostility begets hostility. Confrontation mixed with hostility comes across as an attempt at retribution or punishment.

f. *Confront job-related behavior.* The essential skill to be acquired for constructive confrontation is to translate counterproductive behavior into job-related consequences. These consequences are much easier to deal with than a person's feelings, attitudes, or values. The following two examples illustrate the difference between confrontations that address job-related behavior and confrontations that address personal behavior:

> **Manager to Sales Associate:** [*job related*] I wish you would smile at customers more frequently. They are likely to purchase more goods when they receive a warm smile from the sales associate.

> **Same Manager to Sales Associate:** [*not directly job-related*] I wish you would smile at customers more frequently. If your attitude isn't right, you'll never make a good sales associate.

> **One Supervisor to Another:** [*job-related*] I can't help but overhear you use all those four-letter words. If you keep that up, you may lose the respect of your employees. Then they won't listen to you when you need something done out of the ordinary.

> **One Supervisor to Another:** [*not job-related*] I can't help but overhear you use all those four-letter words. There's nothing worse than a foul-mouthed supervisor.

g. *Show that you care.* Human resource consultant Pamela Cole suggests that you show that you care when you confront.[4] She says, "You have to care enough to confront because it's easier not to confront and to avoid the problem. Caring enough to confront increases the likelihood that the situation will be resolved. When I do not confront a situation, I can be pretty much assured that it will go on the way it is or get worse."

Communicating the fact that you care can sometimes be done by the sincerity in your voice and the concerned way you approach the difficult person. Using the words "care" and "concern" can be helpful. To illustrate, "The reason I'm bringing up this problem is that I care about our working relationship. And I'm concerned that things have been a little rough between us."

3. Give Ample Feedback

The primary technique for dealing with counterproductive behavior is to feed back to the difficult person how his or her behavior affects you. Focus on the person's behavior rather than on characteristics or values. If a *repulsive type* is annoying you by constantly eating when you are working together, say something to this effect: "I have difficulty concentrating on the work when you are eating." Such a statement will engender less resentment than saying, "I find you repulsive, and it annoys me." Giving feedback is part of confrontation.

4. Listen and Respond

Closely related to giving feedback is to listen and respond. Give the difficult person ample opportunity to express his or her concerns, doubts, anger, or other feelings. Then acknowledge your awareness of the person's position.[5] An example: "Okay, you tell me that management is really against us and therefore we shouldn't work so hard." After listening, present your perspective in a way such as this: "Your viewpoint may be valid based on your experiences. Yet so far, I've found management here to be on my side." This exchange of viewpoints is less likely to lead to failed communication than if you judgmentally state, "You really shouldn't think that way."

5. Criticize Constructively

Feedback also sets the stage for criticism. It is best to criticize in private and to begin with mild criticism. Base your criticism on objective facts rather than subjective impressions. Point out, for example, that the *yes-person's* lack of follow-through resulted in $10,000 in lost sales. Express your criticism in terms of a common goal. For example, "*We* can get the report done quickly if *you'll* firm up the statistical data while I edit the text." When you criticize a coworker, avoid acting as if you have formal authority over the person.

6. Use Tact and Diplomacy

Tactful actions on your part can sometimes take care of annoying behavior by coworkers without having to confront the problem. Close your door, for example, if noisy coworkers are gathered outside. When subtlety does not work, it may be necessary to proceed to a confronting type of feedback.

Tact and diplomacy can still be incorporated into confrontation. In addition to confronting the person, you might also point out a strong point of the individual. In dealing with a know-it-all you might say, "I realize you are creative and filled with good ideas. However, I wish you would give me an opportunity to express my opinion."

7. Work Out a Deal

A direct approach to dealing with problems created by a difficult person is to work out a deal or a negotiated solution. Workers who do not carry their load are successful in getting others to do their work. The next time such a worker wants you to carry out a task, agree to it if he or she will reciprocate by performing a task that will benefit you. For working out a deal to be effective, you must be specific about the terms of the deal. The worker may at first complain about your demands for reciprocity, so it is important to be firm.

8. Reinforce Civil Behavior and Good Moods

In the spirit of positive reinforcement, when a generally difficult person is behaving acceptably, recognize the behavior in some way. Reinforcing statements would include "It's fun working with you today" and "I appreciate your professional attitude."

Think It Through   **The Nightmare in the Logistics Department**

Larry Smits was happy to join the distribution department of his company as a logistics specialist. His position centered on keeping track of shipments to customers and from vendors. A distribution specialist works extensively with computers to track shipments, but part of the job description involves telephone and face-to-face contact with company insiders and outsiders. Larry enthusiastically explained his new job to his girlfriend: "Here's a great opportunity for me. I'll be using a sophisticated software system, and I'll have lots of contact with a variety of people. I'll be talking to marketing executives, purchasing agents, truckers, package-delivery people, and office assistants. Equally good, I'll be learning about a very important part of the business. If the company doesn't ship goods to customers, we can't collect money. And if we don't receive shipments of supplies that we need, we can't produce anything ourselves."

During the first four months on the job, Larry's enthusiasm continued. The job proved to be as exciting as he anticipated. Larry got along well with all his coworkers and developed his closest friendship with Rudy Bianchi, a senior distribution specialist. Rudy had several more years of experience than Larry and said he would be willing to help Larry with any job problem he encountered. One day Larry took Rudy up on his offer. Larry was having a little difficulty understanding how to verify the accuracy of tariffs paid to several European countries. Part of Larry's job was to make sure the company was paying its fair share of tariffs, but no more than

Continued

necessary. Larry sent Rudy an email message asking for clarification on three tariff questions. Rudy answered promptly and provided Larry with useful information.

When Larry next saw Rudy in person during lunch, he thanked him again for the technical assistance. "No problem," said Rudy. "I told you that I'm always willing to help a buddy. By sharing knowledge, we multiply our effectiveness." Larry detected a trace of insincerity in Rudy's message, but later thought he might be overreacting to Rudy's colorful way of expressing himself.

Several days later Larry was reviewing a work assignment with his supervisor, Ellie Wentworth. She said to him, "How are you coming along with the problems you were having understanding how to verify tariffs? That's a key part of your job, you know." Larry explained to Ellie that he wasn't having any real problems, but that he had asked for clarification on a couple of complicated rates. He also pointed out that he quickly obtained the clarification he needed. Larry thought to himself, "Oh, I guess Ellie must have misinterpreted a comment by Rudy about my clarifying a few tariff rates with him. I doubt Rudy would have told our boss that I was having trouble. Why should I be paranoid?"

One week later Rudy stopped by Larry's cubicle. At the moment, Larry had the classified ad section of the *Los Angeles Times* on his desk. "Are you job hunting, Larry? You're a rising star in our department. Why look elsewhere?"

"I'm not job hunting," said Larry. "I was just curious to see what kind of demand exists for logistics specialists. It's just part of my interest in the field. It's reassuring to know we're part of a growing profession."

"That's a great answer," said Rudy. "I was just pulling your chain a little anyway." A week later Ellie was reviewing some work assignments with Larry. As the discussion about the work assignment was completed, Ellie said, "I think highly of how you are progressing in your job Larry, but I want to make sure of one thing. Before we give you another major assignment, I want to know if you are happy in your job. If for any reason you are planning to leave the company, please let us know now."

"What are you talking about?" said Larry with a puzzled expression. "I intend to be with the company for a long, long time. I can't imagine what gave you the impression that I am not happy here."

As Larry left the office, he was furious. He began to wonder if someone was spreading malicious rumors about him. He muttered silently, "It couldn't be Rudy. He's supposed to be my friend, my mentor. But I have to get to the root of this problem. I feel like I'm being sabotaged."

Questions

1. What devious technique might Rudy, or another coworker, be using against Larry?
2. What motivation might a coworker have for raising questions about Larry's job knowledge and loyalty to the company?
3. How should Larry deal with his suspicions?
4. How effectively has Ellie dealt with her two concerns about Larry?

Summary

As a coach or mentor, you may sometimes have to help an individual who creates problems for others yet has the skill and mental ability to do otherwise. A short list of the many different types of difficult people include: know-it-alls, blamers, gossips, dictators, repulsives, yes-people, no-people, Jekyll and Hydes, backstabbers, lone wolves, and Chicken Littles. Tactics to use to successfully coach and mentor such problem individuals are (1) taking problems professionally, not personally, (2) confronting the difficult person, (3) giving ample feedback, (4) listening and responding, (5) criticizing constructively, (6) using tact and diplomacy, (7) working out a deal, and (8) reinforcing civil behavior and good moods.

Key Terms and Concepts

Backstabbers	Jekyll and Hydes
Blamers	Know-it-alls
Chicken Littles	Listen and respond
Constructive criticism	Lone wolves
Dictators	No-people
Difficult people	Repulsives
Feedback	Tact and diplomacy
Gossips	Yes-people

Expand Your View

Skill-Building Exercise: Dealing with Difficult People

In both of the following scenarios, one person plays the role of a group member whose work and morale suffer because of a difficult person. The other person plays the role of the difficult person who may lack insight into what he or she is doing wrong. It is important for the suffering person to put emotion into the role.

■ *Scenario 1: The dictator.* A dictator is present at a meeting called to plan a company morale-boosting event. Several students play the roles of the group members. One student plays the role of a group member who suggests that the event center around doing a social good such as refurbishing a low-income family's house or conducting a neighborhood cleanup. Another student plays the role of a dictator who thinks the idea is a bummer. The group member being intimidated decides to deal effectively with the dictator.

■ *Scenario 2:* A no-person. One student plays the role of a worker with a lot of creative energy whose manager is a no-person. The energetic worker has what he or she thinks is a wonderful way for the company to generate additional revenue—conduct a garage sale of surplus equipment and furnishings. The worker presents this idea to the no-person manager, played by another student. If the manager acts true to form, the worker will attempt to overcome his or her objections.

Questions

1. What is the difference between a *difficult person* and a *substandard performer*?
2. Which type of difficult person have you encountered the most frequently on the job?
3. How do you know whether or not you are a difficult person?
4. What do you think are the motives of a person who acts like Jekyll and Hyde?
5. How might humor help you deal with the repulsive type of difficult person? Supply an example of a witty comment you might use.
6. A Xerox executive once said, "You have to be awfully talented to get away with being obnoxious." In what way is the preceding a valid comment?
7. How effectively might punishment turn around the behavior of a difficult person?

Notes

1. Career Track seminar, "How to Deal with Difficult People," 1995; Kenneth Kaye, *Workplace Wars and How to End Them: Turning Personal Conflicts into Productive Teamwork* (New York: AMACOM, 1994); "Tame the Best Within You: How to Cope with Mood Swings in Yourself and Others," *WorkingSMART* (April 1999), 1; brochure for ETC w/Career Track, 3085 Center Green Drive, Boulder, CO 80301–5408.
2. Dru Scott, *Customer Satisfaction: The Other Half of Your Job* (Los Altos, CA: Crisp Publications, 1991), 16.
3. Gary G. Whitney, "When the News Is Bad: Leveling with Employees," *Personnel*, January–February 1983, 37–45; Dot Yandle, "Incivility: Has it Gone Too Far to Fix?" *Pryor Report/Success Workshop*, March 1997, 1.
4. Quoted in Priscilla Petty, "Shortest Route to Good Communication Is Often a Straight Question," Gannet News Service, October 18, 1983.
5. Sam Deep and Lyle Sussman, *What to Say to Get What You Want* (Reading, MA: Addison-Wesley, 1995).

Learning Links

Cavaiola, Alan A., and Neil J. Lavender. *Toxic Coworker: How to Deal with Dysfunctional People on the Job.* Oakland, CA: New Harbinger, 2000.

Eehart, Martien. "Top 7 Ideas for Dealing with Difficult Employees." http://top7business. com/stategies/personnel/19990504.html

Falcone, Paul. "Welcome Back Disgruntled Workers." *HR Magazine*, February 2001, 133–137.

Grensing-Pophal, Lin. "High-Maintenance Employees." *HR Magazine*, February 2001, 86–91.

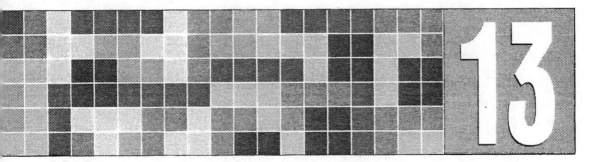

Developing Protégés

PERFORMANCE GOALS

After studying this chapter and doing the exercises, you should be able to:

- select a protégé to mentor.

- select methods for developing your protégé.

- position your protégé for promotion.

"Without you, Max, I would still be working in the call center."

FURTHER UNDERSTANDING MENTORING

As mentioned in the overview at the beginning of the book about the roles of coach and **mentor,** mentoring is a complex activity that involves a greater range of helping behaviors than coaching. A mentor is not only a coach, but a person who is trusted and respected, and a teacher. A stronger emotional tie exists between mentor and protégé than betwen coach and team member. Their relationship is based on compatibility between the two personalities. In fact, friendship is intrinsic to successful mentoring.

Many organizations have formal mentoring programs. However, you need not be a manager to mentor, nor do you need to have a formal mentoring program in place. You need only to have more experience than the person you choose to mentor. Indeed, mentoring traditionally has been an informal way of helping others on the job.

MENTORING EFFECTIVELY

1. Select a Protégé

In preparation for becoming a mentor, it is helpful to think of the type of person you would prefer as a **protégé.** This is an important task because your rapport with your protégé is critical to both your success as mentor and that of the person you are mentoring. A major consideration in choosing a protégé

The following self-quiz will help you think through important attitudes and behaviors related to your willingness to be a mentor. To develop mentoring skills, you need to offer help to several people for at least six months. Not only will you use the coaching skills discussed throughout the book, you will also use the tactics described in the next several pages.

Answer Generally Agree or Generally Disagree to the 10 statements below:

	Generally Agree	Generally Disagree
1. Many times in life I have taught useful skills to younger family members or friends.	☐	☐
2. Few people would be successful if somebody else had not given them a helping hand.	☐	☐
3. I would enjoy (or have enjoyed) being a Big Brother or Big Sister.	☐	☐
4. Experienced workers should be willing to show the ropes to less experienced workers.	☐	☐
5. I would like to be considered a good role model for others in my field.	☐	☐
6. I have very little concern that if I shared my knowledge with a less experienced person, he or she would replace me.	☐	☐
7. At least one of my teachers has been an inspirational force in my life.	☐	☐
8. I am willing to drop what I am doing to help somebody else with a work or study problem.	☐	☐
9. I am willing to share my ideas with others, even if I do not receive any credit.	☐	☐
10. Helping others contributes toward becoming immortal.	☐	☐

Interpretation: This quiz does not have a precise scoring key. However the more of the above statements that you agree with, the more likely you have the proper mental set to be a mentor.

is to look for a good return on your investment by choosing someone who is shows good potential. A person with high potential is likely to benefit more from your advice than is a person with low potential. (If you are strongly humanistic, however, you might want to choose a protégé who needs the most help. A person who needs considerable help might not have such high potential.) If you are intent on selecting a high-potential person, you will probably encounter competition from others in your firm who would also like to mentor the same shining star.

Another key consideration in choosing a protégé is to look for good chemistry (rapport) between you and the person you would like to help. Because a mentor–protégé relationship is based on trust and respect, it is best to mentor someone you trust. A third factor in choosing someone to mentor is to ask yourself, "How can I best help the organization?" With this as your guide, you might choose to mentor a person who would flounder without help and direction. Along the same lines, you might choose to mentor a person who needs help with career advancement. An accounting manager in a telecommunications company chose to mentor a computer programmer who was blind because she thought that this person needed more help in learning the organization than would many sighted workers.

Another consideration in choosing someone to mentor is to choose an individual whose growth and development you care about. If you say to yourself, "I would really like to see this person succeed," you have passed another criterion for choosing a mentor.

2. Develop your Protégé[1]

To help your protégé successfully grow and develop, you will provide the following types of mentoring behaviors.

■ *Coaching.* A mentor gives on-the-spot advice to help the person being mentored improve his or her skills. Develop and practice the skills discussed throughout this book to give you a good foundation for **coaching.** Suppose that you have watched your learner give a PowerPoint presentation. You saw considerable room for improvement. Later that day you have a quick debriefing session and explain: "I know you wanted to get across as many useful facts as possible this morning. The problem is that your slides were so packed with information that most people—including me—were confused. Put less information on each slide next time."

■ *Acting as a referral agent.* The mentor sometimes refers the protégé to resources inside and outside the company to help with a particular problem. For example, the person you mentor might want to know how to get the employee benefits package modified. Or, your learner might want to talk to someone about getting overseas business experience. Because you have a good contact in the international marketing department, you facilitate a meeting between the person you are mentoring and the international manager.

ACTIVATE YOUR SKILLS: Selecting A Protégé

To be a successful mentor it is necessary to select protégés who will respond well to your advice and coaching. Since the mentor-protégé relationship is personal, much like any friendship, one must choose protégé carefully. In about 50 words (in the space provided), describe the type of person you would like for a protégé. Include cognitive, personality, and demographic factors in your description. Indicate why you think the characteristics you chose are important.

My Ideal Protégés

_____

_____

_____

_____

_____

_____

As many class members as time allows can present their descriptions to the rest of the class. Look for agreement on characteristics of an ideal protégé.

■ *Role modeling.* An important part of being a mentor is to give the protégé a pattern of values and behaviors to emulate. Refer to the discussion of being a role model in Chapter 4, "Using Influence Tactics," to review what is expected. The general idea is that your protégé should perceive you as a positive model of the type of behavior that leads to success in your firm—and perhaps other firms. For example, you might describe how you took a company trip and stayed an extra two days to visit family members. You could then explain how you subtracted from your travel and expense reports those costs attributed to visiting family members. You are acting as a role model because you are demonstrating an ethical way of reporting expenses.

■ *Providing acceptance.* A mentor can be helpful just by giving support and **acceptance.** The coaching skills of showing empathy and active listening can help you show support to your charge. Chapter 8, "Encouraging Positive Actions," provides more information about encouragement. For example, if your learner wants to explore the possibilities of an overseas assignment, you might say, "I think you should look into international business. In recent years, many people promoted into executive positions have overseas experience. You are up-to-date in your career thinking."

Suppose the person you are mentoring fails an assignment and has the courage to speak to you about it. You can show acceptance with a statement such as, "I have never known a successful person who did not have to overcome a career setback at least once, so consider this a learning experience."

■ *Counseling.* A mentor listens to the protégé's problems and offers advice. **Counseling** is much like coaching except that counseling deals more with feelings and emotional concerns. For example, if the person you are counseling is angry and upset about her relationship with her team leader, you might let her vent her feelings. In the role of a counselor, you are more likely to ask questions than give direct advice. For example, you might ask your protégé, "What have you done so far to improve your relationship with your boss?" or "Is there anything you might be doing that is triggering anger in your boss?"

A standard practice is for the counselor to reflect feelings in a way similar to the active listening described in Chapter 3. To the angry protégé you might say, "You are angry with your boss," or "Your boss is upsetting you."

■ *Providing a trusting relationship.* A mentor is, above all, a trusted person, and the relationship of trust and respect extends two ways. A *trusted* mentor is one who will not pass on confidential information or stab you in the back. Review Chapters 1 and 2, "Building Trust" and "Showing Empathy," respectively, for more about this topic. The traditional meaning of *mentor* implies that the mentor is a friend of the person being mentored. Today there is less emphasis on friendship, yet trust and respect are still important.

Some mentors have destroyed trust and respect by sexually harassing the person being mentored. A dinner together to discuss career concerns can sometimes drift into a situation in which the mentor makes sexual advances toward the learner. Sometimes the mentor and protégé become romantically involved, but this is not sexual harassment. Sexual harassment refers to unwanted advances.

■ *Encouraging problem solving.* Mentors help protégés with **problem solving** by themselves and make their own discoveries. Refer to Chapter 11, "Helping Others Solve Problems," for detailed information on this behavior. Here is an example of helping the learner solve a problem:

> **Learner:** I'm getting a little concerned. My boss hasn't accepted any of my brainstorms in recent months.
>
> **You:** Why hasn't your boss accepted any of your brainstorms in recent months?
>
> **Learner:** I don't know. She just listens for a few seconds, then shrugs off my ideas.
>
> **You:** How well developed are your ideas?
>
> **Learner:** I'm not sure. I like to be spontaneous with my creative thoughts.
>
> **You:** Could you improve on your idea production?
>
> **Learner:** Maybe I should study a problem more carefully before jumping in with a suggestion. I should present a more thorough plan for solving a problem instead of winging it. Thanks. I'm glad you made me think through the problem.

■ *Explaining the ropes.* A general-purpose function of the mentor is to help the protégé learn the ropes, which translates into explaining the values and dos and don'ts of the organization. For example, the mentor might tell the learner, "It is okay to make a mistake occasionally or to say you do not know. But lying or faking it in this company creates a quick path out the door." Another example is that the mentor might tell the protégé, "In this company numbers count. You have to show quantitatively what you have achieved. The favored people here make their financial targets in sales, cost savings, and turnover figures."

■ *Teaching the right skills.* The original role of the mentor in teaching skills (such as a master teaching an apprentice) is highly relevant today. Among the many skills a mentor can help the protégé develop are those dealing with information technology, customer service, corporate finance, and achieving high quality. An example of a complex skill a mentor might teach is budget preparation. Preparing a budget is complex because it goes beyond learning mechanical routines such as making calculations. The person being mentored might be advised, "It is much better to be liberal in estimating your expenses. Give yourself a little slack. Then when you spend less than you estimated, you will be perceived as prudent. If your spend more than you estimated, you might be perceived as having forecasted poorly." (Notice that this mentor is reasonably ethical. The mentor is not advising the person being mentored to spend all the money in the budget to avoid a possible budget cut in the next years—the philosophy of "use it or lose it.")

3. Position Your Protégé for Promotion

Effective mentoring on the job also involves helping your protégé advance at work or in his or her career. To do so, you engage in very specific mentoring behaviors.

■ *Sponsoring.* **Sponsoring** occurs when a mentor actively nominates candidates for promotions and desirable positions. For example, if asked to nominate a coworker for a promotion to supervisor or team leader or for a special assignment, a mentor will frequently suggest his or her protégé.

■ *Protecting.* A mentor might shield a junior person from potentially harmful situations or from the boss. For example, the mentor might tell her protégé, "In your meeting today with the boss, make sure you are well prepared and have all your facts at hand. He is in an ugly mood and will attack any weakness."

■ *Sharing challenging assignments.* One member of the team does not ordinarily give assignments to another, yet in some situations you can request that your protégé help you with a difficult task. You would then offer feedback on your protégé's performance. The purpose of these high demands is to help your team member develop more quickly. (In this scenario, the mentor is a team member rather than a higher-ranking person.)

■ *Developing an action plan.* The purpose of an **action plan** is to specify in writing the steps your protégé should take to achieve his or her goals in relation to the mentoring. The action plan develops a path for attaining a goal such as enhanced visibility in the company or new skill development. A typical issue is how the protégé can become better known in the company, thereby enhancing his or her chances for better assignments and promotion. You work jointly with the person you are mentoring to develop a realistic action plan. The action plan also serves as a reminder of steps the protégé should be taking to achieve an important career goal. Figure 13.1 presents an action plan worksheet for gaining visibility.

Action Step	Date Accomplished	Result or Comment
Mentor recommends protégé for task force assignment	January 5	Task force on investigating potential ethical violations was eye opener. Met a few key executives who praised my work.
Join racquet ball club	February 7	Played mostly with people my age, but now play about once a month with senior marketing executive. Have established good rapport with the executive.
Volunteer to interview at career fair	March 1	Exciting opportunity. Enjoyed representing the company. Director of human resources now knows I exist and that I want to help the company.
Take short course in international marketing	April 1	Course was entered into company skills bank. Managers in the company now know I am serious about receiving overseas assignment.
Nominate self for team leader opening	May 1	Best move so far. Will be the next team leader in my unit when present team leader's term expires. Now on the road to the executive suite!

FIGURE 13.1   Action plan for attaining increased visibility.

Dawn Albright is a sales representative for an office-supply company. She has five years of successful experience selling furnishings and interior designs to business firms in her area. Dawn worked her way up from taking telephone orders for small supplies such as computer paper, print cartridges, pencils, ballpoint pens, and pencils. By the fifth year of her employment, Dawn became the highest producer in the office.

One day Dawn's manager, Jim Bastian, requested a favor: "Dawn, would you be willing to take Marilyn Lake under your wing? Marilyn is the newest member of the sales staff. I think she could benefit from the guidance of a real pro like yourself." Dawn enthusiastically agreed to assume responsibility for becoming Marilyn's mentor. She told Jim, "I sure could have used help myself when I was getting started."

Jim explained to Dawn that Marilyn might need a lot of help. He pointed out that the company was taking a chance on placing Marilyn in a sales position. Jim's reasoning was that although Marilyn made a professional appearance, she didn't appear to have much self-confidence. When Dawn asked Jim to give her a few specifics, he commented: "A lot of little things have given me the impression that Marilyn needs more self-confidence. When I interviewed her, Marilyn could not give me any example of how she had ever been a leader in anything. Also, when I ask her opinion about almost anything, she says, 'I'm really not sure' or 'I don't have an informed opinion.'"

Dawn later met with Marilyn to explain that although she was not her boss, she had volunteered to spend time showing her the ropes. Marilyn expressed appreciation and acknowledged that she had a lot to learn about the business.

Dawn began working with Marilyn by taking her along on visits to a few of her best accounts. Dawn even allowed Marilyn to receive credit for the sale of a few desks, chairs, and coffee tables because she assisted in the sales. Over the next several months, Dawn would discuss Marilyn's sales progress with her from time to time. The two would discuss Marilyn's tactics and the plans she formulated to develop each account. Marilyn listened attentively and followed Dawn's advice carefully.

Toward the end of the sixth month of their working relationship, Dawn received a telephone call from Marilyn late one night. Marilyn pleaded with Dawn to accompany her on a sales call to a potentially big account. "I know that if you are present at this meeting, between the two of us we will close the sale," said Marilyn.

Dawn's first thought was that Marilyn needed the experience of closing a big sale herself, yet she obliged. "Marilyn has a point," thought Dawn to herself. "Experience is a big factor in closing such a large account. And our firm could sure use the business."

As the months rolled by, Marilyn made an increasing number of requests for Dawn's advice on sales tactics. Twice more she pressured Dawn into helping her close big sales. Dawn

Continued

hinted that Marilyn should close the sale herself, but Marilyn insisted that she needed help just one more time.

Soon Marilyn began to seek Dawn's advice on matters outside work. One day Marilyn asked if Dawn would help her choose a dress for an engagement shower. Another time Marilyn sought Dawn's advice on how she should handle her parents' negative reaction to her latest boyfriend. Soon Marilyn was telephoning Dawn at least twice a weekend, asking to discuss questions about both work and her personal life.

Finally Dawn thought to herself, "My being a mentor to Marilyn has gone too far. I'm her confidante, her big sister, and her sales consultant. At times I also feel I'm her mother. This relationship is draining me."

Questions

1. How effective is Dawn as Marilyn's mentor?
2. In what way might Dawn be hindering her protégée's development?
3. What should Dawn do about her relationship with Marilyn?
4. What underlying issue might Dawn be neglecting in dealing with Marilyn?

Summary

Mentoring is a complex activity that involves a variety of helping behaviors, all related to being a trusted friend, coach, and teacher. The relationship between mentor and protégé is stronger emotionally than that between coach and team member and is based on friendship. Although some companies have more formal mentoring programs, mentoring is generally informal.

The process of developing a protégé involves (1) selecting a protégé; (2) working with that protégé through coaching, acting as a referral agent, role modeling, providing acceptance, counseling, providing friendship, encouraging problem solving, explaining the ropes, and teaching the right skills; and (3) positioning the protégé for promotion through sponsoring, protecting, sharing challenging assignments, and developing an action plan for that protégé.

Key Terms and Concepts

Acceptance	Mentor
Action plan	Problem solving
Coaching	Protégé
Counseling	Sponsoring
Friendship	Training

Expand Your View

Skill-Building Exercise: The Anxious Protégé

One student plays the role of Pat, a purchasing specialist in the materials management department of a large company. Another person plays the role of Chris, Pat's mentor, who is a manufacturing manager with 10 years of experience in the firm.

Pat schedules an appointment with Chris to discuss career concerns. Pat is visibly upset and anxious and says to Chris, "You're my mentor. Help me. Do something for me. I'm stuck in a rut, spending most of my day making online purchases for the company. I enjoy being part of B2B [business to business online purchasing], but I feel I'm headed nowhere. I've followed your advice about building a network, but all I have achieved is a handful of receipts for taking people to lunch. I thought a mentor was supposed to look out for my best interests."

Chris wants to be a good mentor and help Pat but thinks that a realistic discussion is needed about what a mentor can and cannot do.

Two pairs of students role-play for about 10 minutes. The rest of the class provides feedback on Chris' skill in being an effective mentor. Jot down the specific comments you think are constructive.

Questions

1. If you were to have a mentor (or do have one), what roles would you want (or do you want) that person to play?
2. If you were choosing a mentor or protégé, to what extent would the person's gender be an influential factor?
3. Describe any barrier to good performance you have encountered. How might your supervisor have helped?
4. Would you be comfortable with having a mentor several years younger than yourself? Explain your reasoning.
5. Would you be comfortable with having a mentor of the opposite sex?
6. In what way might a person use email to foster a mentoring relationship?
7. Many people today hire business coaches to act as their mentors, frequently paying about $300 a month. What is your opinion of the return on investment from hiring a professional mentor?

Notes

1. Based mostly on Kathy E. Kram, *Mentoring at Work: Developmental Relationships in Organizational Life* (Glenview, IL: Scott, Foresman, 1985), 22–39; Erik J. Van Slyke and Bud Van Slyke, "Mentoring: A Results-Oriented Approach," *HR Focus*, February 1998, 14.

Learning Links

"Coaching/Mentoring/Knowledge Sharing." http://humanresources.about. com/cs/coachingmentoring (accessed December 6, 2003).

Thomas, David A. "The Truth About Mentoring: Race Matters." *Harvard Business Review*, April 2001, 98–107.

Van Collie, Shimon-Craig. "Moving Up Through Mentoring," *Workforce*, March 1998, 36.

Wild, Russell. "The Best Career Advice I Ever Got." *Working Woman* December–January, 2001, 77–80.

Index